FIGHTING
THE NEXT GOOD FIGHT
BRINGING TRUE BROADBAND TO YOUR COMMUNITY

Craig Settles

This publication is designed to provide accurate and authoritative information in regard to the subject matter covered. It is sold with the understanding that the publisher is not engaged in rendering legal, accounting, or other professional service. If legal advice or other expert assistance is required, the services of a competent professional person should be sought.

ISBN-13: 978-1-58776-905-4
Library of Congress Control Number 2010924477

Manufactured in the United States of America

1 2 3 4 5 6 7 8 9 10 NetPub 0 9 8 7 6 5

HUDSON HOUSE PUBLISHING

675 Dutchess Turnpike, Poughkeepsie, NY 12603
www.hudsonhousepub.com   (800) 724-1100

Contents

Forward

Broadband is critical to our future but it is not an end in itself. It is a means to a variety of ends, both direct and indirect, that can play a major role in improving our communities and our quality of life. Bigger, faster and more affordable broadband will improve educational opportunities and help better prepare our students to compete in a 21st Century global economy. It will help improve the quality of healthcare, while reducing the costs of providing services. It will make our government more transparent, and facilitate the ability of citizens to interact with and participate in the development and administration of public policy.

Better broadband will help our nation address energy goals. Smart grid technology depends upon it. Also, if even a small percentage of American workers have broadband capacity at home that allows them to telecommute for one day a week, we can significantly reduce vehicle miles traveled, lessen the stress on our public transportation systems, and reduce the emissions that result from our daily commutes.

Broadband is also all about jobs, jobs, jobs. We hear and read about it daily on the news, from political leaders, and from the talking heads in the media. So many of today's jobs require significant bandwidth, and this demand will only increase for the jobs of tomorrow. But our communities can't access that bandwidth today. When every community in the United States has access to broadband capacity that we need, workers won't have to leave small towns and either move or commute to more urban communities for work. As a former mayor, I can attest to the direct benefits that shorter commutes have in local communities. Every hour that a worker is not traveling to or from a job, is an extra hour that one can spend with family, be involved in a service club, volunteer at a faith-based institution, coach little league, volunteer in our schools or so many other similar activities. These are the small things that add up to improve the quality of our communities and our lives. And broadband is a means to achieving these ends.

The United States has fallen behind much of the rest of the world in broadband deployment and usage. We have to do better. To be successful, every person and every interested entity has a role to play. We will not achieve our broadband goals if we wait for the private sector to solve our broadband problems. To be sure, the private sector has an important role to play in improving broadband in the United States. But the public sector, and especially local government, also has a critical role, and indeed a responsibility to be involved. Community input is vital, as our government organizations must be responsive to the needs and desires of local citizens.

Craig Settles understands these issues better than most. He understands the challenges that our nation faces as it considers our broadband future. He understands the critical roles that government must play as leaders and as facilitators in our efforts to plan, deploy and effectively utilize broadband in the United States.

Craig has been involved in these issues for some time, and he has witnessed the problems that many have faced in trying to determine and implement a positive community role in broadband deployment. This book does more than explain the issues and highlight the goals. It is filled with helpful suggestions for how to address community broadband issues and how localities can take their role in broadband deployment to the next level. What issues should be explored at a foundational level, what communities need to be engaged, how do we develop a plan that can be successful and move it forward to successful implementation? This book defines the issues, identifies the pitfalls, lays out the options, and ultimately prepares you to structure your own plan to promote better broadband in your community.

Addressing a community's broadband needs, developing a strategy for improvement, and implementing it successfully is not an easy process. Like anything worthwhile, it will take significant time, effort and a lot of hard work. There is no one size fits all, correct way to effectively improve broadband in every community throughout the nation. The beauty of this book is that it provides a tremendous source of background information, an opportunity to learn from the mistakes and the successes of others, and provides an important foundation for anyone interested in promoting broadband in their own community.

Ken Fellman
Arvada, Colorado
President, National Association of Telecommunications Officers and Advisors (NATOA)

CHAPTER 1

Now Is the Time for Broadband

As of this book's final editing, not much of the $7.2 billion in broadband stimulus money has flowed out of Washington, D.C. At least all of the states and the District of Columbia are moving down the path to receiving a few million of that for broadband mapping. However, in one very important way the stimulus was a roaring success for 2009.

More people are talking about, and planning for, broadband Internet access than ever before. Broadband seems to be talked about everywhere. You see it in intensive media coverage, from the largest business and technology publications to smallest local newspapers. It seems everyone is aware of and concerned about the United States' dismal standing in the world for broadband availability, speed and price. More importantly, communities nationwide are planning to bring better, faster broadband to their areas even if they don't get or try to get stimulus money.

The broadband stimulus threw a white-hot spotlight on the burning need in the U.S. for broadband that's measured in megabits and gigabits per second. As to be expected, the stimulus also threw hundreds of local and regional governments, service providers, consulting firms and digital speculators into a frenzy to apply for this money. However, it is neither the media coverage nor the race for "free" money that makes broadband a technology imperative all communities should be considering. In the watchwords of the first Clinton for President campaign, "it's the economy, stupid!"

It's Always Been About Money

Almost any way you look at it, economic development is the big driver of efforts to make broadband a reality in communities. Whether delivered exclusively by service providers, built by communities through the government or public utilities or midwifed by some variation of a public-private partnership, broadband is mainly about constituents' economic wellbeing. In a period where many local economies are in the dumps, broadband is seen as the path to a reversal of fortune.

Broadband offers tangible benefits, such as enabling local businesses to compete more affectively at home and abroad, instilling new marketable skills among current and future workers and reducing the costs of providing government services. Small businesses in urban areas are hard pressed to survive depending solely on struggling inner city economies, and challenged trying to expand into national or international markets. Affordable broadband access is a definite lifeline for businesses. Companies in small towns and rural areas are isolated from many resources typically found in large cities, so they need to a good Internet access or they will be tempted to move to where they can get it, further crippling communities.

Another factor influencing communities of all sizes is the effort to retain talented workers. Cities and towns with great college communities are finding that keeping these graduates around, or attracting graduates from universities in other cities, is increasingly difficult if the work and living environment aren't what grads have come to expect. The average college grad these days has been weaned on smartphones, text messaging, social networks and broadband everywhere. If businesses want to attract this budding workforce, it helps to operate where the communication infrastructure meets these workers' needs.

A deeper concern than retaining workers is the plight of low-income urban and rural communities that struggle to get their youth proficient in just the basics of reading, writing and arithmetic. The ability of preparing these students to compete with a global workforce that's computer proficient is yet another level of need that tears at the economic fabric of communities. Broadband is our best hope for an equalizing force that equips teacher, student and parent to become partners in creating a digitally literate, financially independent, worldly wise, upwardly mobile workforce.

What professionals say about broadband and economic development

I surveyed 260 economic development professionals in December 2008 for a research report sponsored by the International Economic Development Council (http://www.successful.com/msp/snapshot-12-08.pdf). Two key questions this report addresses are 1) how can citywide and regional broadband networks impact economic development, and 2) can broadband facilitate personal economic development and entrepreneurship within underserved communities.

I asked those professionals who work in cities and counties that have broadband networks to indicate specific results they can tie to the technology. I started with the impact of wireless networks.

If you have an area-wide wireless network that businesses can access, how has it affected economic development?

	Definite impact	Indirect impact	Too soon to tell	No impact	Difficult to measure
New businesses moved to your area	13.9% (16)	12.2% (14)	25.2% (29)	19.1% (22)	29.6% (34)
Existing businesses have stayed	13.9% (16)	18.3% (21)	19.1% (22)	20.9% (24)	27.8% (32)
Local companies more profitable	11.6% (13)	13.4% (15)	25.9% (29)	16.1% (18)	33.0% (37)
More tourists	4.4% (5)	9.7% (11)	28.3% (32)	22.1% (25)	35.4% (40)
Increase in events (conventions, fairs)	2.7% (3)	9.8% (11)	25.9% (29)	32.1% (36)	29.5% (33)
Revitalized depressed business areas	6.1% (7)	10.5% (12)	30.7% (35)	26.3% (30)	26.3% (30)

( ) = number of respondents

Figure 1

It is interesting to note in Figure 1 that a similar number of respondents find wireless networks have a direct and an indirect impact on bringing and retaining businesses in an area. However, those who feel wireless has an indirect impact on drawing tourists and special events is noticeably larger than those who find wireless has a direct impact. At one point elected officials cited the ability to attract tourists and events as main reasons for building WiFi networks. The numbers in the survey, as well as a similar survey I conducted in 2007, do not prove out this claim.

Wired networks (see Figure 2), on the other hand, are far and away the bigger inducements for businesses to locate into an area, with nearly three times as many respondents saying wired networks definitely impact location decisions as those who say the networks indirectly influence these decisions. Depending on the business, this may be the number one issue that can seal the deal–or kill it if broadband isn't available.

If you have an area-wide wired network that businesses can access, how has it affected economic development?

	Definite impact	Indirect impact	Too soon to tell	No impact	Difficult to measure
New businesses moved to the area	32.0% (41)	12.5% (16)	20.3% (26)	16.4% (21)	18.8% (24)
Existing businesses have stayed	26.0% (33)	22.0% (28)	14.2% (18)	15.7% (20)	22.0% (28)
Local companies more profitable	23.2% (29)	18.4% (23)	18.4% (23)	14.4% (18)	25.6% (32)
More tourists	5.6% (7)	12.7% (16)	20.6% (26)	27.8% (35)	33.3% (42)
Increase in events (conventions, fairs)	5.7% (7)	13.0% (16)	20.3% (25)	32.5% (40)	28.5% (35)
Revitalized depressed business areas	9.6% (12)	13.6% (17)	24.8% (31)	27.2% (34)	24.8% (31)

( ) = number of respondents

Figure 2

Whether directly or indirectly, wired networks also appear to have a greater impact on current businesses and businesses moving into an area than wireless. Separate interviews with North American cities and counties show that these networks have a similar impact on commercial entities from all industries, as well as nonprofit and not-for-profit organizations.

The drop-off in the impact that wired networks have on drawing tourists and special events to an area is similar to the drop-off with wireless. Wired networks, though, do have a greater direct role in revitalizing distressed business areas than wireless networks. It could be because fiber network projects have had a longer time to mature in communities. A greater percentage of respondents feel the benefits of wired networks are easier to measure compared to respondents with wireless networks in their areas. Also, a smaller percentage believes that it is too early to tell what benefits wired networks deliver.

Looking at the big picture of economic impact, you already know that your ability to improve the financial wellbeing of your business community has a direct impact on city revenues, the local job market and the personal economics of the general population. If one of your community's missions is to draw new businesses into town, or to keep existing ones from leaving, your communication infrastructure and how you enhance it can be an ace card for you to play. When setting your objectives and evaluating the value of broadband to your area, carefully examine how implementation and use of the technology will influence which businesses stay, grow, come or leave.

Ground-level view of broadband's impact

After getting a quantitative view that confirms broadband has both direct and indirect impacts on economic development, it's good to get some in-depth views of those working in the trenches. The following individuals represent a cross section of U.S. communities that have wired or wireless broadband networks.

Casey Beard · Dir, Emergency Mgmt Dept, Morrow County, OR	This rural county has a 1,500-mile combination WiFi and fiber network they hope eventually to expand through a 10–18-county regional effort
Brian Feist · Emergency Services Director · Cambria County, PA	Cambria County trumped the state's anti-muni wireless law to build a countywide network consisting of several licensed and unlicensed wireless technologies
Brent Graden · Dir of Economic Development, Prestonburg, KY	This rural community of 4,800 initially built their Meraki WiFi network to increase shoppers downtown, and now the network is citywide
Terry Huval · Dir of Utilities–Lafayette Utilities System	Lafayette, LA, a city of 125,000, repelled incumbent telecom attacks to build a fiber network offering 10 Mbps symmetrical speed, $28/month, 50 Mbps, $58
Michael Johnson · VP of IT and Broadband, Jackson (TN) Energy Authority	This public utility for the Jackson, a city of 75,000, built and operates a fiber network with 16,000 subscribers, 20% of which are businesses
Scott Martin · Dir of Commerce and Leisure Services, Sandie Terry, IT Director · Franklin County, VA	A 721 square-mile community of 50,000 people, Franklin County partnered with a local wireless Internet access provider (WISP) to build a countywide fixed wireless network using unlicensed spectrum
Mark Meier · CIO, Oklahoma City	A 550-square mile Tropos WiFi network covers this city that has both typical urban and remote rural sections within its borders
Jory Wolf · CIO, Santa Monica, CA	Wolf's IT department started with no funds and created a citywide fiber network that built up a $2.5 million capital budget from cost savings to the city, and service revenue

Here's what they have to say about broadband's economic impact on their respective communities.

FEIST (CAMBRIA COUNTY):

We see a twofold economic benefit. Customers get cost savings from traditional service providers using the network, along with more reliable service; the county government gets revenue from network services providers buy to pay for the system and eventually enhance the network. So far we haven't seen an economic development impact on businesses. Our biggest influx of customers is residential because we just started recruiting ISPs that offer business services.

JOHNSTON (JACKSON, TN):
We calculate $8 million in direct benefits coming from the lower prices we give customers compared with other communities. We have new businesses starting up, and some such as those in the high tech industry expanding. Several industries list fiber as a strong draw for them to locate in Jackson. However, it does take some time to achieve these benefits. Some benefits are intangible or unpredictable as more things come online that people want to take advantage of, such as social networking.

MARTIN/TERRY (FRANKLIN COUNTY):
Everything we're doing is the reverse of the norm of calculating specific numbers for economic impact, such as 400 jobs created, or 100 businesses coming to town. It's difficult for a staff our size to easily track this kind of data. We ask, does broadband help college or high school students do well in their studies, does it allow people to purchase homes at the lake and work from there? We look at the many examples these questions uncover and determine that the network is a success. The value of broadband is real to us. Since we built the network we're the fastest growing county in Virginia.

Broadband is a big factor in attracting businesses. We're recruiting data centers that are between half-billion and billion-dollar projects. A new data farm might bring 50–60 jobs with $75,000–$100,000 annual salaries. The buildings built for them are assets, and the equipment used represents significant tax revenue every 18 months when they upgrade and replace the technology.

GRADEN (PRESTONBURG):
We made broadband the central part of an integrated package of activities to revitalize business in our downtown. Our wireless network, combined with 3% loans and development efforts for buildings that weren't being used, made downtown friendly for businesses. Wireless created incentives for people to come downtown.

Within three months of launching the network, 22 businesses moved in with 40–45 new jobs. This creates a cyclical effect with more people coming into downtown, which attracts more businesses. Tax revenue from here in the first year of the program went up $111,000, mostly through new business growth. This in turn allowed us to buy an aerial fire truck, which has kept property owners and government insurance rates from rising.

MEIER (OKLAHOMA CITY):

The existence of the WiFi network allowed us to do things not otherwise possible. We created 42 locations with research quality weather stations to collect all kinds of weather data since we have such a high number of tornados. The University of Oklahoma has projected a $50–$100 million economic impact over 10 years because of the 'Mecca effect' as scientists, weather forecasters, organizations and conferences from all over the world visit. These people will be staying in hotels, eating at restaurants, taking tours and so on.

There are a whole lot of small benefits too. We increased attendence in city events since staff sells tickets with mobile devices and wireless cash registers. Inspectors give instant licensing approvals, which save several days of construction time for projects. But WiFi did not create this. WiFi created the opportunity and eventually these benefits happen. Fiber is completely different. Wireless probably won't supplant it as the preferred technology because the expectations for fiber are greater.

BEARD (MORROW COUNTY):

Our farmers started benefiting as soon as the network was completed. They access data while in their vehicles in the fields to track market conditions and make decisions to buy or sell commodities immediately to maximize their profits. They also check the weather to increase or decrease irrigation flow.

When farmers find signs of distress or bugs, they take pictures and wirelessly send them to a university to get input on how to deal with the problem and minimize damage. The network enables them to check crops' shipping status or determine which grain elevators to send them to, plus use RFID to track equipment and better manage equipment maintenance. Farmers quickly became more competitive nationally and internationally.

WOLF (SANTA MONICA):

The most significant impact for government and community-based organizations is that our broadband lowers their cost of doing business because they're saving a bundle of money on expensive, outmoded communication technology. Operating our network costs 35% of what we used to pay for very slow T1 lines and frame relay. We couldn't support video or other high-bandwidth apps such as the traffic advisory system and traffic cameras we have now.

For businesses, their overhead drops significantly when they lease dark fiber from us and get discounted bandwidth services. Hospitals transport high bandwidth videos and data so doctors make critical decisions in just two or three minutes. Hospitals collect money faster.

These benefits happen relatively soon after fiber is turned on. We can deploy faster and more efficiently than carriers. They have approval processes for new services and prices that take around three months. We can piggyback off of public works when they're doing street resurfacing and putting in new sewer lines to reduce construction costs.

Economic Development Is Personal

When reading about the economic development impact of broadband, you obviously hear a lot about the technology impacting business constituents. But what about your individual constituents? They also are, or should be, key beneficiaries of the intersection of broadband and economic development initiatives.

A significant number of communities assessing the value of broadband see it as a way to close the digital divide between disadvantaged individuals and the rest of the community. Whether it's in urban or rural communities, public policy makers want to make it possible for lower income and geographically isolated people to become proficient using Internet technologies to advance themselves. Economic development professionals in my survey share this viewpoint.

Respondents are quite bullish on broadband's potential to foster entrepreneurship (see Figure 3). One approach that's sure to remove individuals from public assistance rolls is to enable them to create and manage a business using the Internet for global outreach, even if these are one-person ventures run from their homes. 71% feel it's quite likely or possible to use broadband to increase start-ups among low-income constituents. A sizeable percentage (20%) also realizes that to make this work, some entity must provide assistance such as training and mentor programs.

Can a municipal or community broadband network influence individual entrepreneurship among underserved constituents (low income, elderly, rural)?

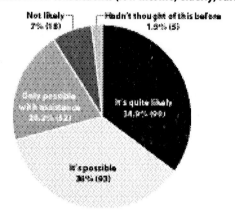

I found a similar percentage of economic development professionals also view broadband as a potent tool to help current and future workers (youth) develop the digital skills required to better function in a technology-dominated global marketplace. Just over 68% (see Figure 4) believe broadband is key to aligning workers with future employer needs. You will be hard pressed to improve existing local business or attract new businesses without such a workforce.

Can the use of muni or community networks help effectively prepare and/or re-train the workforce in underserved areas for better jobs?

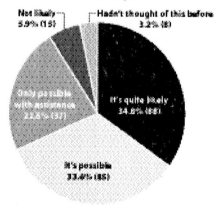

On this issue too I want to present some "in the trenches" perspectives. I interviewed these individuals for my supplement to the economic development survey report, "Assessing What Our National Broadband Strategy Should Be (http://www.successful.com/msp/snapshot-1-09.pdf).

Bob Cabeza · Exec. Dir YMCA Downtown, Long Beach, CA	Mr. Cabeza manages a program that teaches youth nationwide high-end digital media skills through neighborhood tech labs, and then connects those skills to academic achievement and workforce development
Ron Dickerson · Economic Development Manager, MTCO Corp.	This independent local exchange carrier develops and delivers services that help communities in their region, which is near Peoria, IL, attract business and expand existing businesses.
Stephane Gallant · Dir. Of Operations, NEOnet	This regional organization partners with private sector businesses and secures grants to bring broadband networks to rural and remote areas of Ontario, Canada where there is not highspeed access.
Greg Goldman · CEO, Digital Impact Group	Formerly Wireless Philadelphia, this nonprofit entity continues to carry out the citywide network's original mission—bringing underserved constituents into the digital economy through access, hardware, training and key partnerships.
Karl Robillard · Mgr, Employment Programs/Tech Lab, St. Anthony Foundation, San Francisco, CA	This nonprofit organization runs technology training programs that help low-income individuals enter, re-enter and/or advance in the workplace.
Wes Rosenbalm · President & CEO, Bristol Virginia Utilities, Jerry Brown · Exec. Dir., Bristol Office of Economic Development	This public utility has built its fiber optic network out to over 65% of the homes and businesses in Bristol and surrounding area of 20,000 people.
Jeff Rossate · Business Development Division Administrator, Iowa Department of Economic Development	This agency promotes policies and practices that improve the state's economic progress.
Dan Speer · Exec. Dir., Pulaski-Giles County (TN) Economic Development Council	Mr. Speer was the driving force of this city and county project to bring municipal-owned fiber highspeed access to every home in the county
Esme Vos · Founder, President, MuniWireless.com	Ms. Vos has been a long-time expert, champion and extensive knowledge resource regarding municipal broadband issues and activities

These broadband leaders see a significant up-tick in home-based businesses as a result of broadband. They also support using broadband as a primary vehicle for re-training your workforce to meet digital opportunities and challenges. Realize that the broadband technology and applications you put in place to facilitate re-training and distance learning for adults possibly can be modified for your youth population. In some cases, it may be the youth you should work with first, then have them train the adults.

GOLDMAN (PHILADELPHIA):

We've identified partner organizations dedicated to this objective that seed home businesses with capital and training. Many don't have a digital component, so we provide it. It's similar to what we do with individuals in welfare-to-work programs. The service groups have done the pre-screening, they have people in classes, and clients have completed the business training. We give them the technology package of computer, software, Internet access and training. Sometimes we identify funding for the technology, in other cases the organizations solicit funding.

SPEER (PULASKI):

We believe the future of economic development is in what's called economic gardening, meaning you teach people entrepreneurial skills such as bookkeeping and business development. Then you show people opportunities in the knowledge industry, for example, that they can take advantage of from home using broadband. We're doing this now during the downturn, but if it's successful we may continue when things pick back up.

ROSENBAUM/BROWN (BRISTOL):

Certainly the networks can lead to more home-based businesses, but that is a difficult outcome to track. In my opinion, another potential outcome is more telecommuting. As costs increase for businesses such as utilities, energy and travel, the networks may allow people to work from home and be just as productive, if not more so, than they are from 9:00 to 5:00 in an office environment.

DICKERSON (MTCO):

I have friends who makes as much as a schoolteacher's salary selling over eBay. You see a lot of that these days. Be careful about zoning issues, though. Some places put you through a special-use process with city council that can be unnecessarily restrictive.

ROBILLARD (SAN FRANCISCO):

The biggest workforce re-training trend we see is with men over 40 whose entire working life has been in physical jobs such as construction, farm labor and the like. They know their body's going to wear out if they stay in their jobs. Broadband can lead them to plenty of service jobs in low-income areas. For example, we have so many single-room occupancy buildings in the city we can send people with computer skills to be desk clerks and create a new economy.

CABEZA (LONG BEACH YMCA):

Community tech centers in which our youth teach adults have a large part to play. Some people are not comfortable going to a college where there appears to be a big monstrosity of bureaucracy because they don't know how to navigate the system. These tech centers build trust because they have a cultural connection to the community. We're a go-between for parents and traditional schools, so people trust our resources

ESME VOS:

For most classrooms today to do any serious re-training, they need broadband. People have to get online to find or exchange information and discover options even before they can begin training. And they need total time flexibility getting access in order to be effective because some may have temporary jobs or young kids. People who are planning these programs have to think outside the box in terms of how they deliver re-training because times are so difficult.

GALLANT (NEONET):

The nice thing about community colleges is that they're in tune with the local economy and can adapt course to meet those needs as broadband is implemented. One of the things you have to deal with, though, is that people who need re-training are often technology illiterate. So first offer courses on how to use technology, which makes it less intimidating. Make sure the necessary instruction you need to give people transfers well to the online environment.

To Sum It Up

Broadband's impact on economic development is a very important consideration when deciding if you're going to pursue building a network and the weight of all of the associated tasks. But it isn't the only factor influencing the "go, no-go" decision. Using broadband to enable telemedicine applications, improve government operations, increase public safety operations and enhance energy conservation and management can hold equal or greater sway.

This first chapter emphasizes economic development because the economy is what's on quite a few people's minds. You can use economic development to motivate a broad range of potential stakeholders to actively take part in the network's planning, implementation and even the financial participation. At the same time, there are specific constituencies that may find additional motivation in these other purposes for the network.

In the following chapters, I describe needs analysis tactics that help you determine what are the main drivers for broadband in your specific community. When you use these tactics to examine who can benefit from broadband and how, you should see a clear and comprehensive picture develop of how to proceed with creating your broadband plan. As your broadband plan takes shape, the number of stakeholders who literally buy into that plan should increase, which is good politics and great risk reduction.

CHAPTER 2

Defining the Strategic Goals for Broadband

In my high tech marketing/PR heyday, I swore by a book titled "How to Get Your Point Across in 30 Seconds or Less" by Milo Frank.

In just over 120 pages you get a blueprint for crafting and delivering a persuasive 90-word (30-second) statement that tells people what you want and why. Those pursuing broadband projects of any sort would benefit greatly by reading this book.

This isn't a creative writing or business presentation lesson. I'm suggesting how you protect your broadband project from the Achilles heel that could hobble many who are involved with broadband efforts, whether they are private sector companies, broadband grant applicants, federal agencies or local governments. The inability to succinctly and effectively state the mission of your broadband project could severely limit your project's ability to get off the ground, or the chances of reaching its goals if it does move forward. The process of creating an accurate, motivating vision statement is also how you define effective broadband strategic goals.

The Vision is the Mission

I read quite a few of the summaries of the 2,200 proposals submitted to NTIA/RUS for possible broadband stimulus funding. Read any 10 and you'd be hard pressed to find one 90-word blurb that by itself answers the key questions, 1) what does the applicant plan (want) to do, 2) what will the network achieve and how, 3) why is their approach better and 4) how will they financially sustain the network? Each community is different with distinct technology needs, yet does one of these applicant's summaries say something markedly distinct from the 1000 proposals before or after it?

You may wonder why this matters. It matters because thoroughly researched answers to these four questions determine whether, and to what degree, your broadband project will succeed. The 30-second, 90-word summary of these answers is your vision for the broadband project. A well-articulated vision entices money besides from sources stimulus grants, inspires sweat equity from stakeholders and keeps the network project team focused on the things that matter.

To put the value of vision statements in context, President John F. Kennedy articulated this vision in 1961: "I believe that this nation should commit itself to achieving the goal before this decade is out of landing a man on the moon and returning him safely to the earth." In July of 1969, the first man walked on the moon and returned safely to the earth. This simple mission statement that produced awesome results is only 31 words.

Though much is written about the value and virtue of a good vision statement, its real power comes from the process by which you distill a complex technology and the facets of its deployment down to 90 words or less. I spoke with someone who worked with several stimulus grant applicants, and feels people who can't write a good summary statement probably don't have all the information needed to develop a good plan. There are project teams and stakeholders who don't fully understand the benefits of broadband, so they intend (hope) to sort that out later if they receive a grant. For those trying to secure budget funding or commercial financing, you likely don't have this luxury. You'll have to do the legwork upfront.

So how do you get from here to there? Let's say your goal is to create a vision statement that results in a broadband network that accomplishes the equivalent of taking you to the moon in eight years. You first need to spend time working on getting the answer to those four key questions I posed. It requires a lot of critical thinking, initial planning, some problem solving and idea generating.

Once you formulate reasonable answers, and accept that these answers will evolve as you move through the various stages of planning and deployment, you have to do more critical thinking to get to your vision statement. In some ways coming up with an effective summary is a more intense cerebral exercise than uncovering the answers, and usually requires many people participating in the process to come up with the right words.

"Know what you want"

Mr. Milo's book presents several steps to creating your 30-second message, but one in particular is critical to making your case for a broadband implementation: know what you want.

If you don't know or can't coherently articulate an answer to the burning question "what do you want," chances are your project faces an uphill battle to get funded, or to be successful if it is. Who has the clearer vision, the project team that intends "to deploy a shovel-ready, sustainable, licensed microwave Middle Mile to WiMAX wireless broadband Last Mile network to provide broadband services in a service area comprised of six counties…?" Or the team that wants to "bring fiber optic service to over 47,000 homes, 7,000 businesses and 200 anchor institutions in 9 underserved Indiana rural communities [and] create an expected 270 plus new jobs?"

You may want to build a network and convince a lot of people to the use broadband, or just achieve a somewhat limited objective such as creating a few dozen public computer centers and set up local libraries and schools with Internet access. In either case, Milo says "know what you want." The main hooks in a summary or executive statement are, what do you want to do with broadband, what do you want to accomplish, how will people's lives subsequently be better?

This issue of knowing what you want covers all aspects of broadband, and extends to everyone influencing broadband locally or nationally. Headlines in Fall 2009 asked why do we need $100 million to do broadband mapping? Earlier in February that year, the stimulus bill set aside $350 million for states to develop maps. But what was it that the government, underserved communities or private sector companies wanted to accomplish that requires maps? Despite the fact the government eventually figured it might get the job done for 2/3 less money, which should have been the headlines, something's missing if the media was still questioning the money's mission seven months later.

The exercise of probing, pondering and distilling the answers to "what do they want" down to 90 words could have inspired a quite compelling vision. Just as important, a good vision statement might have resulted in a different approach than spending that much money or limiting eligibility for receiving this money to only nonprofit organizations. Maybe the strong vision would have justified the full $350 million.

In Chapter 6 I tackle the issue of broadband maps and what the vision should be. However, for now let's just say that "we need good maps to get a good broadband strategy" is not quite the vision statement to make a lot of people feel warm and fuzzy about spending several hundred million dollars. More importantly, I don't believe it's the right vision.

Vendors and service providers are not immune to the challenges posed by not knowing what the vision is. For them, creating effective broadband networks comes down to getting in sync with what prospects need or want, or helping those prospects figure out what they want. Conversely, communities can't get broadband networks into their areas without some sort of private sector involvement, but life could be difficult if no one's sure what the private sector players want from the relationship besides money.

Moving from the complexities of technology, community interests and politics to a simple but powerful vision is rarely quick and is often difficult, yet the payback is huge. As I said earlier, once you do the critical thinking about a project that leads you to write an effective vision statement, you are more likely to plan and implement an effective broadband project.

Gotta Know Up from Down with Your Broadband Sustainability Strategy

Once you get settled on a vision, it's time to think about strategy. There may be many strategic objectives you wish to achieve with your broadband project: improve the delivery of local government services, boost economic development, close the digital divide in your community. I will touch on these throughout the book. However, there should be one overarching strategic goal–ensure the financial sustainability of your network.

Whatever it is you do with it and whomever you serve with it, the broadband network has to generate enough revenue, grants or money from other sources that pays the bills. That's what ensures financial sustainability of the network. It costs money to build and operate networks, buy or create the various broadband applications and develop the content that has to run on the network so people and organizations are motivated to use it. Private sector entities involved with these networks have the added pressure of stockholders, boards and banks to financially satisfy.

If the heart of your broadband network's sustainability strategy is selling subscriptions to individual residents and general mobile consumers, you should re-think your plan. Were the network a house, this is similar to fixating on making a classy roof or cool playroom while ignoring the strength of your foundation.

Starting with the hype-heavy days of muni wireless, community broadband projects have been plagued with this concept that individual subscribers are the main base for sustaining a network. Residential subscribers collectively are important, but they are the secondary consideration. Why are they not the foundation of the network? In areas most in need of broadband, individuals are often too few in number to offset the price of the network, the costs of winning and keeping them is huge and there are financially superior alternatives. This last factor, superior alternatives, can lead to 60%, 70% or more of your network's revenue.

Go for the gold, add the silver

The stimulus program has put the broadband grants needs of unserved or underserved populations front and center. However, many of those lacking adequate service live in small towns and rural areas, and/or they have low incomes. In each community that's a small universe of potential paying subscribers for network buildouts that come with six-, seven- or eight-figure price tags. Furthermore, only a portion of these universes will become paying customers since not everyone who can afford service wants to pay for it, at least initially.

The cost of winning and then keeping individual subscribers is a major pain in the assets. Yeah, you can quickly snag that low-hanging fruit, people who currently have no access and desperately want it or despise the access they do have. But you have to spend money to win everyone else as customers, maybe $200 or $300/person that take months to recoup. Collecting monthly payments isn't cheap, and tech support is expensive. There's customer churn too, since competitors won't sit still while you rake in the bucks. They'll raise the heat. So you have to drop prices, offer incentives, bring lost customers back to the fold.

Smart cities go after financially superior alternatives, and consider individual subscriptions bonus bucks. Towns such as Fredericton, New Brunswick in Canada bring the largest local businesses into a room and convince everyone to chip in to underwrite the network buildout and operating costs. Each business gets superior broadband service for a cheaper price than incumbents were going to charge. Or you can imitate Santa Monica, CA's focus on selling fiber services to local businesses that churn much less than consumers.

Another tactic is to use broadband to convince two or three major businesses to move into the area bringing significant dollars and other benefits. Lafayette, LA was able to seal the deal with a major call center operation that brought 600 jobs to the community thanks to their fiber network. The center benefits the network directly as a customer, and the community economically with new jobs and taxes.

The bottom line is this. Individual subscribers can comprise a quality roof on your house of sustainability. But the financial foundation lies with government use of the network to cut its operations costs and with your leading businesses. They're solid, they don't require much (relatively) customer support and once satisfied they rarely churn. Other institutional customers such as medical facilities and colleges are the sturdy walls that hold up your roof. And a fresh generation of broadband-stimulated home-based businesses provides financial insulation.

Here's an important side note. Building your sustainability strategy by initially focusing on institutional rather than individual customers helps avoid some of the spitting contests over networks such as Wilson and Salisbury NC were forced to have with conservative think tanks and incumbent astroturf organizations. These groups are generally PR pawns funded by large telco and cable companies to fight community broadband projects. If you come to the table and slap down a dozen memoranda of understanding from prospective institutional subscribers, your network plans are much less vulnerable to opponents' charge of being fiscally risky.

Strategic Thinking Beyond the Network

One downside of the broadband stimulus program is that it has limited a lot of communities' and private sector companies' focus to building a physical infrastructure. When you read the media coverage, city councils' proclamations that broadband is equivalent to gas and water and so on, you get the clear impression that it's all about access. "Once we have access, [fill in the blank] will improve." However, the network's value and financial sustainability do not rest solely with the access, but also with the applications and services the access enables. Therefore your strategic thinking must encompass question #2 raised earlier, what do I do with this beast once I finish building it? What do I want to achieve and how will we do it?

If you presume to know what constituents want or need to do with the network, you'll often be wrong. As a result, the network may not be built with enough capacity or the right technology, it may not be properly marketed once it's built or it could fall victim to any number of other shortcomings that limit your success. In diverse communities, the various constituent groups need different content, services and applications.

The wants of individual subscribers seem to evolve or totally change every 6 to 12 months and depend a lot on consumer trends. With institutional customers, they tend to lock into a relatively small set of applications they want to use (e.g. data warehousing, mobile workforce management, video conferencing). Their data trafficking and quality of service needs may be very demanding, but they tend to remain constant for one or two years, maybe longer.

To put the proper post-buildout strategy in place for the network, you have to execute a needs assessment process that is very intense, inclusive and ongoing. During the assessment, focus on what people want to do on the network so you can decide what infrastructure should be deployed. Within the confines of budget, though, you need to build the network with attention to how it's going to be used five years from now as well. You want to cast a wide net for gathering feedback with lots of feet on the street, plenty of constituent meetings and a few town hall events.

Once the network is built, you need some sort of feedback-gathering mechanism that keeps a finger on the pulse of your various constituent groups so you keep your operations strategy current. Maybe you can rely on service providers and vendors to do this as part of their responsibility to upgrade the network, or turn to the stakeholders you identify through the tactics I discuss in later chapters.

Your institutional network customers can be responsible for gathering feedback from their own employees, and pass results on to you. Whichever feedback-gathering methods you settle on should be determined by the nature of your community and the constituents involved with the project, and the methods should be flexible.

Getting to long-term strategic thinking

One of the biggest challenges for both public and private sector organizations involved with broadband is trying to predict and adequately plan for the future. Unless you have a great crystal ball vendor, there are so many unknowns when using technologies that change as fast as Internet-related infrastructure and applications. One strategy that communities can consider is to focus on building the middle mile infrastructure and let others such as private sector companies build the last mile and deliver applications directly to consumers.

In case the term middle mile is new to you, often used with its companion "last mile," think of a broadband network as the Mississippi River and its tributaries. The mighty Mississippi hauls a huge amount of water between Lake Itasca in Minneapolis to the Gulf of Mexico. At numerous places along the river, tributaries run out from the river into communities. The last mile of a broadband network, similar to the Mississippi's tributaries, is the infrastructure where consumers, businesses, et al attach to the network to send and receive data, Web content, e-mail, etc. The network middle mile is the Mississippi itself. The middle mile moves data from any number of communities and constituents.

The broadband stimulus program has made middle mile projects a big topic of discussion because: 1) you can't have a broadband network without some sort of middle mile infrastructure hauling data back and forth between network customers and the Internet; and 2) even though it costs a lot to build, you can make broadband available to communities without needing to build or sell current and future technologies that touch customers. Operationally, someone else carries the expense of keeping the customer satisfied through last mile infrastructure, applications, customer support and new features.

Cambria County, PA is a good example of how to proceed with a network project if a community decides to go with this middle mile strategy. They wanted to build a network primarily for public safety, and to also enable all of the towns and townships in the county to have valuable Internet access. However, the county didn't want to be in the business of serving end users directly.

Cambria county's story

In Pennsylvania, Cambria County overcame restrictive legislation by using the telco's own anti-muni network rules to build a county-owned middle mile network that moves beyond public safety to impact education, economic development and digital inclusion. Planners of the 700 square-mile network, which has been up and running since June 2008, used the following approach that I believe you will see become the foundation for many projects.

For a brief bit of background, Verizon and Comcast lobbied Pennsylvania legislators to pass a restrictive anti-muni network bill in the face of Philadelphia's plan to build a citywide wireless network. The law says any local government must present to the incumbent telco (Verizon) plans for a network they want. If the incumbent refuses to build the network to spec as presented, the community can move forward. Verizon could agree to build the network, thus killing the community's right to own it, but Verizon would have to build the network within a year. In this case, Verizon let Cambria County have at it.

The county thus created a network infrastructure with features developed to withstand the rigors of public safety use (e.g. must-have-24/7 reliability, redundancy, disaster recovery). Once you build a network with that much power, there is tremendous excess network capacity for other uses.

They incorporated into the infrastructure multiple wireless technologies (5.8 GHz, 900 MHz, 4.9 and WiFi), and support for other wireless technologies such as WiMAX, SCADA and automated meter readings. This gives the last mile builders and service providers great flexibility in being able to use a technology that best meets their respective customers' needs.

The county generates various cost savings by reducing or eliminating telecom service contracts so they can receive these services through the network, therefore recovering much of the money they spent to build the network. If you identify one or two key uses for the middle mile infrastructure that allows you to recoup costs, you're in a strong financial position to facilitate last-mile capabilities.

Cambria County offers the network infrastructure as a digital "turnpike" to their 62 municipalities, enabling those munis to deploy applications and services that meet their respective needs, rather than trying to sell everyone the same package of applications. The latter was the fatal flaw that led to the demise of a major Silicon Valley, CA regional network project. The organizers could never get 44 municipalities to agree to funding a set of services the planners wanted to offer.

Along with Conxx, the county's vendor that manages the network as a contractor, officials offer Cambria County schools a package of services that enable them to now provide education and training that prepares the local workforce to function in a digital economy.

The county and Conxx recruited service providers to lease the network infrastructure to providers that are selling services to general consumers that offer faster speeds and lower prices than previously available, if highspeed access was even a possibility. Note that this fo cus on the general consumer comes *after* ensuring the network's financial sustainability through services to local government and other stakeholders.

Since the initial service providers are mainly consumer focused, the county launched a second wave of recruiting to bring in providers that offer business services that further accelerate economic development. This, along with the retraining of the local workforce, is bringing new businesses into the area.

Here's something very important to note. Because each of these services used by the county or offered by them to their various constituents directly saved money or generated revenues for the county, financial institutions literally lined up to offer Cambria County financing. This is a local government attracting investments that some private sector companies trying to deploy similar networks have been unable to do.

Here's a Radical Strategy Idea

Let's explore a different strategic approach to funding.

In 2009 I came across National Community Development Services, Inc. (NCDS), which specializes in boosting the economic health of communities through a process they term economic development fundraising. Their president, Tom DiFiore, and I co-hosted a Webinar on broadband strategy because I believe a process that can raise $1.6 billion over 30 years for projects that spur economic development deserves a fair review by those of us in broadband. We decided to join efforts in the broadband arena.

The concept is simple, really. Rather than look for customers to buy services or charitable donors to contribute to a network, build a financial sustainability strategy based on a campaign to recruit investors for the network. Furthermore, these investors are to come from within the community or communities building the network. We're not talking investors as a euphemism for "subscribers," but people who invest more than the price of service in exchange for a piece of the action. This aligns with my position that communities need to treat broadband networks as a business venture.

The investors in this scenario are community hospitals, large businesses and other organizations I described earlier as institutional customers, but they're putting a financial stake into the project. "Key funders have a greater sense of ownership in the initiative they are funding," explains DiFiore. "An *investor* expects a return on his or her investment, but here, benefits the community receives are the primary return. Broadband creates economic growth, prosperity, and vibrancy for a city, county, or region. The largest stakeholders in a community's wellbeing, therefore, are logical potential investors in that mission, even if they are not customers on the network."

The premise behind NCDS's service is that you should view any community project that improves economic development directly and indirectly as a business venture. Some "x" amount of money goes into the venture. When the investment is successful, return on the investment is more revenue, higher profits, more jobs, a more skilled workforce, improved infrastructure, friendlier business climate, etc. If municipal budgets, bond financing and traditional financing are available or practical for supporting the project, then you turn to those in the community with capital and the greatest stake in the project's success. Since a network offering services to constituents is a revenue-generating business, there is potential for a direct financial return, though as is the case in Fredericton, this revenue is reinvested in the network.

A typical scenario might be to create a co-op or other nonprofit entity. If we use Fredericton as an example, they created a budget for how much it would cost to build and operate a high-end fiber network. They brought together the heads of 12 of the larger commercial and educational organizations from the community and proposed that each of them and the city invest a fairly proportioned amount into the co-op. The co-op then retained contractors and hired personnel to build and operate the network. The investors received broadband services as a benefit while profits from revenues went back into network services that benefit the community, including free citywide wireless.

Putting the economic development fundraising strategy into play

I've truly simplified the start up process since the business, legal and tax procedures to structure the entity are just a little complex, but I want you to grasp the basic concept. DiFiore provides more detail on how the fundraising process would work.

"Most successful fundraising campaigns for community and economic development initiatives usually adhere to four core principles:

1) It's about the *community's needs*–not the organization's needs. So you make the community and the benefits they'll receive from broadband the focus of the campaign, not the organization.

2) It's much easier to raise big money for specific initiatives and projects [digital inclusion, workforce retraining programs, improving healthcare delivery] than it is to fund an "organizational budget." No one is interested in ensuring an income stream for an organization. They want outcomes in the community–not 'activity.'

3) What they help write, they will help underwrite. Key stakeholders and funders must have a sense of ownership in the initiative being funded. The best way to achieve that is to involve them during planning and development.

4) The initiative must be *relevant* to the community's needs and opportunities; there must be *measurable* goals that define progress and success; and the leaders of the organization/initiative must be *accountable* to the investors.

I would also add that "market testing" the initiative through a feasibility analysis to determine the community's likely level of support is absolutely critical."

Since an economic fundraising campaign for investors should bring in some organizations that for one reason or another may not become customers of the network, and possibly wealthy individuals as well, pay attention to the messaging you use.

"I would guess that most people–even smart business people–don't really understand all of the benefits and impacts that a robust broadband infrastructure can bring to a community," states DiFiore. "A new interstate highway or a new industrial park, they understand. But bandwidth, redundancy, etc. may not mean much. Help prospects connect the dots between broadband and community growth and prosperity, then translate this to their own business. When they see the connection, they'll understand the need to invest to make sure it happens."

When DiFiore and I first spoke, one of my concerns was how do you raise the kind of money in this manner that a typical network costs if your population is small. "We've raised millions of dollars for small, rural communities with populations as small as 10,000. The fundamentals are really the same, just on a smaller scale."

He believes that if there's a way to facilitate growth and prosperity, the people and organizations with the biggest potential to benefit should carry a significant portion of the load, with smaller stakeholders providing fair and proportionate levels of support. In Fredericton, with a population of 51,000, there are now over 30 investors of all sizes in the co-op.

"In a large metro area, you might have as few as 80–100 investors supporting a $20 million economic development initiative," says Di-Fiore, "with the lead investor giving two or three million dollars and the top 10 after that giving $9 or $10 million collectively. A small county may launch a $2 million initiative with a lead investor at two or three hundred thousand dollars and the next ten giving around $900,000 collectively."

The other key factor, especially in smaller communities is to execute these programs as public-private partnerships, the kind of relationships I've promoted for years, but the difference is that the private-sector partners are all local businesses. City and/or county government can usually come up with 30-40% of what's needed for these kinds of initiatives, lessening the funding burden for local businesses. Don't forget to include your local banks in the mix. You and your stakeholders can decide if and how you want to work service providers and vendors into the equation.

To Sum It Up

Bringing meaningful broadband to your community is a significant challenge that, when effectively met, transforms the way your constituents live, work and play in ways we are just beginning to see. To achieve these great benefits that broadband promises to deliver, you must develop and articulate a vision that is simple in purpose and clear in direction, yet powerful enough to motivate a diverse array of stakeholders to join in the endeavor. That vision is your mission. As you work through this book and its lessons, don't lose sight of your mission.

That was my 30-second message on the importance of developing a good vision statement to get broadband done.

CHAPTER 3

Who Are the Stakeholders?

There are two groups integral to the success of a broadband project: the project team and the stakeholders.

The project team, which I cover extensively in the next chapter, is comprised of those individuals driving the day-to-day business of planning, needs assessment, engineering, building and possibly running the network. I use the term stakeholders to reference those are representatives, often on a steering committee, from constituent groups directly impacted by the network: local governments, schools, businesses, healthcare facilities and so forth. Stakeholders are also all of the people and organizations that make up the constituent groups that use the network.

Depending on the project, stakeholders may be on the project team in various capacities. At the very least, the project team and stakeholders should meet frequently. To run the best possible needs assessment, stakeholders almost always should be directly involved in this process, though the project team leader should actively manage it. Some of your stakeholders, such as the local hospitals or the largest businesses, may be partners (often referred to as anchor tenants or customers) on the network, meaning they invest a major financial stake and significant input into the network buildout and its operations. As part of their investment they may get network access benefits and other perks.

Identifying Your Stakeholders

It is important early on to determine who the stakeholders are. They have an important role to play providing feedback, gathering research information, overcoming political and financial barriers, rallying constituent support and ultimately recruiting network users (a.k.a. increasing broadband adoption).

This chapter gives a high-level view of the players and their roles. As you consider what organizations and constituents are potential stakeholder, remember to factor in which ones also may be good partners in the broadband project.

It's through your needs assessment that you identify and recruit stakeholder organizations that bring revenue and subscribers to the network. Two main selection criteria should be: 1) who can make you more appealing to federal agencies, financial services companies and other institutions that can bring financing to build the network, and 2) which stakeholders can help you financially sustain the network once it's built. An emphasis on financial sustainability absolutely should not eclipse low-income constituents as key stakeholders who have an equal place at the table. As I mention frequently, by ensuring your network's financial wellbeing you ensure its ability to benefit unserved and underserved constituents.

Besides the agencies giving out broadband stimulus money, the Department of Homeland Security is a good candidate for grants if your stakeholders include public safety agencies. The business community may top your list of partners that can draw support from associations such as the Chamber of Commerce, which in turn can attract smaller business that need a lot of broadband and will pay for premium (but fairly priced) services.

Two powerful county government partners are public safety and public works. Meeting their needs opens your grant options to additional federal agencies such as the Departments of Justice and Energy. Public works projects allow you to reduce the cost of broadband infrastructure build-outs. Every Department of Transportation road, bridge and public building project is an opportunity to install broadband infrastructure at a reduced cost.

K-12 schools, colleges and universities are valuable stakeholders. They have a huge need for broadband, which opens them to various foundation and government grant opportunities. Higher learning institutions that are able to access many megs or gigs of Internet speed are eligible for large research grants that bring huge economic benefits to your community.

Finally, your pursuit of key partnerships should include to the vendors and service providers who make network infrastructure and services possible. However, public/private partnerships need to be better structured than those arrangements highly touted during the days of muni wireless hype. For one thing, no one this time expects private sector companies to carry the whole financial load while the municipality gets free services.

"You have to be sure they can make money," observed Franklin County, Va., IT Director Sandie Terry. "Our wireless Internet service provider has just a two-year return on investment because they're receiving space on vertical assets such as government buildings in exchange for charging local government lower rates." Everyone coming to the table–and I encourage lots of partnering with local or regional telcos and WISPs–needs to be out-of-the-box thinkers when it comes to structuring mutually beneficial partnerships.

Local Governments—Top of the Stakeholder Lineup

Local governments are one of the main entities you want on your stakeholder team. They are or should be the center of planning and development wherever broadband is deployed. They are the community, meaning they represent all of the constituents of a community: businesses, schools, nonprofits, workers, retirees, everyone in all constituencies.

To varying degrees, you find within local government ranks those who can open doors to the constituency groups whose support you need for an effective broadband network. They have clout to make resources available that you'll need for the network, such as telephone poles and water towers for hanging wireless network radios and dark fiber cable. They often have contacts to the leaders within stakeholder groups who you want to play a major role in network business planning.

Local governments also have burning communication and business operation needs for speed that broadband networks can meet better than those of telecom companies. Minneapolis, MN is a prime example. They see enough value in wireless broadband that they committed $10 million over 10 years to be the anchor tenant on US Internet's citywide network.

Debunking the Myths about Government-Run Broadband

I am unabashedly, unashamedly and totally unequivocally in favor of municipal-owned broadband, and networks for which local government is the lead in a public-private partnership. So when exploring the role of government at stakeholders in these projects, the option of their ownership is definitely a consideration that's in play. There are many reasons, but reason number one is, if you want broadband to serve the public good, your chances are much higher with public ownership.

The public discovered soon after the deadline that quite a few of the 2,200 NOFA applications were from local governments and public utilities. Much more than I'm sure some people expected, given how much critics belittled these proposals. It's the usual baseless "government can do no right" you hear when the big incumbents start to quake at the prospect of real competition.

We are well past the time for Federal agencies, policy makers at national and local levels of government and the average citizen on the street to seriously embrace and encourage the role of local government and their constituents in broadband. We've let the lie that governments can't run effective networks fester and poison the broadband discussion.

According to the Fiber to the Home Council's October 2009 report "Municipal Fiber to the Home Deployments", "not a single muni FTTH system has failed. Nationwide, the take rates for retail municipal systems after one to four years of operation averages 54 percent. This is much higher than larger incumbent service provider take rates, and is also well above the typical FTTH business plan. Deployments usually require a 30–40 percent take rate to 'break even' within planned payback periods."

The Council has at least 55 member municipalities and public utilities that run fiber networks. There are municipal-owned wireless networks with services for the general public, and though these tend to be limited-reach networks that cover downtown areas and some retail districts, Allegany (Maryland) and Cambria are two countywide wireless networks. In addition, there are a couple of dozen cities and counties such as Providence, RI, Corpus Christi, TX, New York City that have city-use-only wireless networks covering up to 500+ miles. Local necessity and the stimulus should result in the start of many more government-run networks.

To address why these network make sense, let me tackle three myths about pubic-ownership of broadband.

Myth 1. Government shouldn't be in the business of running broadband networks. People who own the problem of poor broadband access and have to live with the solution should be the primary drivers, if not owners, of programs and policies that impact broadband. I talked to a service provider once who was pretty proud of the fact he could make broadband available in an area without having to work through local government. But he couldn't figure out how to increase his revenue. One solution: partner with those governments and stakeholders he'd been avoiding who represent big-bucks service contracts.

When you read details on successful public retail (opposite of government-use-only) networks, note how many have the city or county government as a principle customer in addition to being the operator. Local government is a customer in need of adequate broadband technology solutions to make its business operation more efficient. Furthermore, local government is responsible for the wellbeing of its commercial, nonprofit and individual constituents, and thus it's going to care more about meeting their needs than a private sector provider that answers first to stockholders.

Myth 2. Government isn't capable of running an effective and/or profitable network. As I mentioned, success stories abound. Cedar Falls, Iowa funded their initial $8 million investment with bonds, and paid the bonds back not with taxpayer dollars, but through revenues the fiber network generated. Franklin County, VA's , a public/private network is one of the fastest growing businesses in its county. Santa Monica, CA started with no budget and now had over $2 million in capital that the network generated through revenues from business services.

Myth 3. Incumbents need protection from unfair competition because local governments have tax and tax levying advantages. Besides the oxymoronic position of arguing that the same local government that can do no right can also be a feared competitor, two other factors dispel this myth. Some incumbents are at a disadvantage not due to tax disadvantages, but because some of them are off the marketing mark with both message and product offering. Others are at a disadvantage playing in the same ballpark as local governments because their technology is lacking. Besides years of observing the communications industry, I've consulted for four service providers and carriers. Two of them suffered from the former shortcoming, and the latter shortcoming hindered the other two.

Incumbents, the Feds and many communities cannot break their focus on individual subscribers as the financial Holy Grail for broadband- marketing strategies, revenue projections and government policies are locked into this worldview. Two former clients could have better fought off the disasters that consumed them had they re-packaged, and then aggressively marketed the same services to businesses and local governments.

As for technology capabilities, one of my favorite stories I love to tell this year is about Wilson, NC. They launched their own fiber network last summer that's offering symmetrical speeds of 100 Mbps to residents and up to a gig per second to businesses. The best that Time Warner Cable can muster is 10 Mbps, for which it charges about $20 more than Wilson's service of the same speed.

Time Warner tried to get a bill passed in the state legislature this year to prevent cities from offering broadband service. They claimed community networks create an un-fair playing field. Personally, if I ran a bezillion dollar company and a small town of 48,000 with no prior technology business expertise built a network 10 times faster than my best offering, I'd be embarrassed to be associated with the bill. If incumbents want to level the playing field, maybe they should out-source their engineering operations to Wilson.

As you line up your stakeholders, definitely put the government on your "Must Have" list. And at least strongly consider putting plans on the table for community-driven network projects.

Gates Foundation May Have Linchpin to National Broadband Strategy

[This is an excerpt from an October 17, 2009 column I wrote for business-technology media Web site GigaOm]

The Bill & Melinda Gates Foundation sent analysis data to the FCC postulating that $5–$10 billion could install fiber networks in most of the anchor institutions (hospitals, medical facilities, schools) in the U.S. These are institutions could be your potential network partners as well as stakeholders. At the time, my strategic mind pondered a question that should always be near the top of people's thinking on broadband: does wiring 98,400 (80% of all U.S. institutions) that lack Net access make good business sense?

The premise behind the Foundation's report–wire of all these institutions first and great things will happen–in my view is a great strategic approach to reap broadband's promised benefits. It should be the core for our national strategy plan, and definitely be a central strategic consideration for communities pursuing broadband. In one fell swoop you resolve three critical issues: financially sustaining the network, fostering economic development and generating widespread broadband adoption.

Financial sustainability

In my assessment, I'm accepting their premise and assuming you're going to build a network business, not just create little islands of fiber access and forget about them. For one thing, money for ongoing operations has to come from somewhere. To make that money, communities do best by integrating their institutions' fiber cabling into one network if possible as part of a single community broadband plan.

If your ultimate objective is to create a communitywide broadband network, then these institutions have to become anchor tenants that actually pay for network services, with libraries being the one possible exception (more on their role in a bit). In many underserved rural and urban areas, low population density and/or low income make it difficult to get enough individual subscribers to pay for a network's operating expenses (OpEx,) even when the network is built mainly on grant money.

If you look at successful networks already in place, anchor tenants collectively produce most of the revenue because each one spends more per month than regular subscribers for services (maybe $1,000, $2,000/month or more) to replace older slower communication technologies, and capitalize on new computing technologies. Extrapolating the Gates premise, if you boost communities' main institutions over the big hurdle of financing broadband buildouts, you make it easier for them to become anchor tenants.

It's important you include local government since it is the mother of all anchor tenants. While it's true that adding local governments would add to the cost projected in the Foundation report, governments can show a significant return on investment to underwrite their portion of the buildout and the OpEx.

Economic development

As your anchor institutions become wired and wireless, they become a catalyst to drive economic development. Santa Monica proved that once a local government and other anchors have a network that's saving or generating money, it's less expensive to extend that network to your largest 10–12 businesses. Word of mouth sells services.

This network extension builds on itself. As infrastructure goes out to the biggest companies, you attract new businesses looking to move or expand to small towns and rural areas. These business subscription revenues help network costs stay reasonable so small businesses in rural and urban areas can afford to tap into the infrastructure. Each anchor tenant can build a wireless hub that attracts shoppers and tourists, which impacts the neighborhood's economic picture.

Broadband adoption

Anchor institutions, particularly when you include libraries in the mix, address one of the more vexing challenges of broadband–getting individuals to subscribe. It can cost hundreds of dollars to win and keep an individual as a subscriber. It's months before each subscriber becomes profitable. Many people have no interest at all in getting on the Internet.

Rather than bust your rump and your budget chasing after these individuals, leverage the anchor institutions. If each institution provides content, services and applications that enable their constituents to benefit without having to fight traffic, stand in line or sit for hours with a phone locked to their ears, individuals will subscribe to the network.

As part of the strategy for broadband adoption, anchor institutions hold the key, so be creative in structuring relationships with them. Libraries especially hold promise in this area because they already are a central point within communities for people who want to use the Net to do research or hunt for jobs.

This discussion, of course, may all be for naught if no one can figure out where the $10 billion is coming from to invest in the anchor institutions. I was hoping Bill and Melinda would round up 9 or 10 of their similarly heeled golfing buddies and put together a broadband investment group. But none of the press articles indicated any such luck. It may be hard to get a second chunk of change out of Congress on the heels of this $7 billion, but stranger things have happened.

A Smart [Grid] Partner for the Broadband Dance

Another stakeholder is the utility company, though public utilities tend to be better suited for this role than private ones because the former tend to be more inclined to work in the best interest of local communities. Years before the stimulus, public utilities from towns as small as Adel, GA (population 5,300) and much bigger cities such as Tacoma, WA (population 196,000) built broadband networks. But things are changing quickly as more utilities move into position to play important broadband partner roles.

[The following is a column I wrote for the rural news Web site Daily Yonder November 11, 2009]

The Department of Energy last month announced 100 stimulus grants totaling $3.4 billion for smart grid projects. Though you may not be familiar with smart grids, the companies poised to start building them offer community broadband project teams valuable partnership possibilities.

Smart grids are the latest technological incarnation of a concept that originated in the 1990's. Instead of having people on foot enduring inclement weather, stymied by locked gates and dodging demented dogs to read residential water, gas and electric utility meters, implement wireless technology to make the job simpler.

Initially wireless devices sat on meters that collected usage data and allowed workers driving down the road to transfer the data to on-board computers, and then to servers when workers returned to the office. This evolved into automated meter infrastructure (AMI). AMI captures data from residential and community "smart" meters without human intervention as frequently as needed, lets you slice and dice this data as granularly as you wish and enables communication from the office to the meters.

These capabilities help utilities cut costs, increase revenue and run better business operations. The two-way communication also enables their customers to receive data better manage their use of water and energy, which helps reduce customers' bills and improves conservation.

AMI inspired utility companies and public policy wonks to dream of creating a smart grid to enhance the standard power grid that directs electric power from several central generators to a utility's customers, and route power more efficiently. Furthermore, there would be devices that plug into customer's power outlets so the smart grid can analyze and manage each appliance's energy use.

The intersection of smart grid and smart broadband advocates

The broadband connection is simple. All of this data flow between meters and utility companies has to move in real time across a highspeed wired or wireless network, and the network has to cover sizeable geographic areas.

In 2007, rural communities such as Milledgeville, GA envisioned building a municipal wireless network to cover the town would support AMI and other applications. City Planner Russell Thompson stated at the time, "hopefully we can tie into the network so it automatically sends readings back from smart meters to our office in City Hall instead of doing walk-by and drive-by readings. As we get it in place, we expect to move into other areas of AMI."

As the smart meter concept gives way to the smart gird, both the geography and number of customers expands tremendously. Whereas Milledgeville had to worry about moving data for only about 4,800 households, the smart grid stimulus grants went to utilities some of which have 500,000 customers and more. Besides those who won grants, another 300 utilities and businesses submitted proposals. I expect many of them to pursue smart grid projects event without stimulus grants.

The potential definitely is there for community broadband to be the data backhaul infrastructure for smart grids. Smart meter devices generally have their data aggregated to another computing device mounted at some location in the neighborhood, maybe one aggregation point per 100 dwellings, for example. Then all of the aggregation points have to traffic their data back to the utility or wherever else it needs to go.

With the grand visions that are unfolding for smart grids, such as moving "green" energy from distant windmill farms to local customers and failsafe provisioning of power in cases when the national power grid fails, the data communication needs intensify. That means relying on fiber (the ideal) or possibly super-fast fixed wireless.

A community's fiber network can provide the backhaul to a regional utility network for aggregated customer data. Or a utility can build its own fiber backhaul and determine how to make that fiber available for local government and other institutions for their use. Many of these stimulus grants went to public utilities, so county governments and local communities should have some influence in a discussion on the matter.

How to leverage the opportunity

Whether your community has a broadband stimulus grant proposal in the works currently, or you are queuing up to apply for round 2 funding, move quickly to determine if your local utility received a smart grid award or was denied one. If your local utility won a grant, meet with them as soon as you can to determine how the broadband proposal you're working on can be tweaked to incorporate, or integrate with, aspects of the smart grid project.

As communities find out they've survived the first phase of cuts in the NOFA funding process, you will soon go into a due diligence phase during which NTIA/RUS may ask you to clarify and fine-tune your proposal. Assuming the utility company is interested in incorporating any broadband infrastructure you build into their smart grid, use that fact to strengthen the financial sustainability of your network by showing the utility as one of your main future customers.

Communities that end up not getting a broadband stimulus grant, should turn the discussion with the utility company around and determine if you can partner and split expenses. Utilities benefit by offloading some of their overhead costs and adding a revenue stream. They, in turn, should have the customer marketing, acquisition and service infrastructure in place to be able to provide these services to those networks run by local governments, nonprofits and public-private partnerships.

Looking at this from yet another angle, some of the 300 utilities that didn't win a smart grid grant should still be motivated to partner with communities that do win stimulus money. With all of the publicity that smart grids are getting, the pressure will be on many utilities to step up to the table and place some sort of bet on the technology. Since DOE's grant required 50% matching funds from everyone applying, you know these utilities have a few chips to play.

Though there are a lot of technology and logistical details that have to be worked out for a partnership of any sort between communities and smart grid builders, there are clearly significant potential benefits that can justify the effort.

To Sum It Up

Stakeholder relationships and partnerships are critical to the planning, operational and financial well being of your broadband project. Communities will assemble a different combination of public and private sector individuals and organizations to play these roles. Early on in your efforts to launch broadband, begin your stakeholder search. In reality, though, this is an on-going process because you should always be looking for those who can advance the cause. You never know where they might come from or what they'll have to offer, but keep your doors open and leave the light on for them to always feel welcome.

CHAPTER 4

Creating a Winning Project Team

I f you want to implement a great broadband network, assemble a great project team with all the right people. Of course, after stating the obvious, the obvious question is "how do I do that?" Governments generally don't have all of the same sticks and carrots commercial entities have to entice and encourage the best and the brightest.

You may be hard pressed to find a universal "right" person or group of people with extensive experience in this area even in the commercial sector given national push to broadband is relatively new, lacking the time to create grizzled veterans. Also, similar to stakeholder groups, project teams reflect communities and their respective needs, so these teams will be different from each other in their composition. However, there are some common threads that will probably identify good prospective candidates.

The internal and external politics of communities, combined with the evolving nature of broadband, require that you assemble a team of individuals with a diversity of skills and social/professional backgrounds. You're looking for people best suited for the tasks and challenges at hand.

You can take a group of volunteer business, education and social service professionals, team them with government professionals, mix in a few consultants and move mountains. The business plan for Philadelphia's initiative, along with relevant research, extensive needs analysis and despite one stormy political battle with Verizon, was developed and presented to the Mayor in three months by a group that had never worked together before planning started. This rivals efforts by some companies backed up with big bucks.

Basic Team Composition

Philadelphia, as a pioneer in the effort to develop large-scale broadband networks with its 143 square-mile network, had to create a lot with no big city predecessors to provide guideposts. Because they executed what I firmly believe was an excellent needs assessment process, particularly under those conditions, I continue to cite their actions as an organizational benchmark when I discuss broadband planning.

Philadelphia's project team that took the city from muni wireless concept to written business plan consisted initially of a leader (CIO Dianah Neff) who presented the idea to then-Mayor John Street and a staff person. When the Mayor gave the go ahead for the project in the summer of 2004, he appointed an executive steering committee of 17 volunteers. The Executive Committee began working on the plan at the beginning of September and presented the finished document to the Mayor in December. Varinia Robinson came on fulltime to the City as a consultant in the Project Manager role and with several other consultants made up the project team. She and Neff served on the Executive Committee, which was disbanded shortly after the plan was completed.

As the project moved along in 2005, a decision was made to create a nonprofit entity, Wireless Philadelphia (now Digital Impact Group), to implement the network plan while keeping much of the business operation free of formal political or bureaucratic ties. The directive that created the nonprofit required there be a board of directors whose members were appointed by City Hall for staggered terms so there would be some government oversight plus some amount of consistency as mayoral administrations changed, yet give the in-coming mayors a voice on the nonprofit. The board then hired a hired fulltime president and staff to run the organization.

Governments that get early clearance and budget approval for project planning may want to set up a nonprofit immediately to let it create all of the necessary staffing structure. Boston set up a nonprofit in 2006, openairboston.net, modeled similarly to Wireless Philadelphia. But in 2007, citywide wireless network projects started imploding due to the bad business models of the companies running these networks. As muni wireless faded from view so did the nonprofit approach to running broadband projects. The broadband stimulus revised this strategy, however, as quite a few nonprofit organizations were created as the formal structure for public-private partnerships to pursue grants, as well as be the project team for broadband implementation.

Larger cities and counties could opt to have a small team at the beginning stages to get the project up and running, and then fold the team into the nonprofit corporation that can decide whether they want an external steering committee. Small cities and towns may create a smaller steering committee than Philadelphia and have consultants or system integrators manage all of the technology logistics. Outsourcing these logistics to consultants avoids having to hire permanent staff and makes things easier if the project started by city staff is later transferred to a nonprofit corporation. The municipal CIO could be tasked with coordinating both groups.

Additional considerations for your project team

There's value in having a larger percentage of the project team consist municipal staff if your network is focused heavily on local government as the main anchor tenant. There's a lot of internal politics involved with getting different municipal departments to work together for this type of project, and "insiders" on the team can help mitigate the challenges. For similar reasons, if most of the network stakeholders are constituents rather than the city or county you want a higher percentage of people on the team representative of those stakeholders.

Each community has to decide what role it wants to have Internet service providers (ISP) and vendors play on the project team. Some municipalities will ask an ISP or local telecom company to come in and run the whole show. Another option, for when the community knows from the beginning it's going to work with a specific ISP or telecom company, is to have them be a member of the team but not lead it.

Possibly a better approach is to invite in several private-sector companies to brief the project team and steering committee on the capabilities and benefits of broadband, let the team do the needs assessment, then invite all or some of the companies back for a chance to participate in the rest of the project. Chose vendors, system integrators and service providers based on which ones you feel comfortable with coming in to take a role. A consulting firm with industry contacts can help identify who's qualified. Ultimately you can decide to not have any vendor or provider participate until you do formal RFPs and select winners.

The Mountain Area Information Network is a multi-county public-owned network in western North Carolina whose Director, Wally Bowen, had to resolve a tricky situation with vendor participation. "A company heard about grants we were applying for to overhaul our network capabilities and sent us materials," recalls Bowen. "We got quite a few free lunches and events that taught us a lot about how technology worked, but we could have gotten locked in with proprietary system had we gone with them. It's good to get in touch with vendors for knowledge, but have to be careful about actually buying."

Bowen is similarly cautious about having private companies be on the project team. He believes you need people on the team who have a passion for the public interest. "If someone seems to be in it for personal gain, this is always a red flag for me. A computer retail store owner came to us, it was clear to he was interested in what's good for community as much as how he could benefit. He brought a lot of technical expertise to the table, introduced us to many important information about wireless technology."

Project teams for regional broadband efforts

As the stimulus popularizes the idea of the multiple counties banding together to pursue broadband, this could change how communities form project teams. On one hand, you can't make the team too large because it then becomes unwieldy and has difficulty managing the variety of tasks involved expediently or effectively. On the other, the group still needs to represent the diversity of stakeholder groups, constituents and municipal governments.

In 2006, several organizations came together hoping to improve telecom infrastructure on Cape Cod, MA, including Cape Cod Community College, the Cape Cod Technology Council and Woods Hole Oceanographic Institution. In 2007, they formed the nonprofit Open-Cape to pursue this goal. OpenCape is driving a regional broadband project to cover over 15 towns and communities in eastern Massachusetts. Here's their approach to structuring the group, which combines project teams and the steering committee. There are four tiers, as described by Board of Directors member Dan Gallagher:

Core Visionaries, Leadership, and Workers. This is the OpenCape Board of Directors Executive Committee. These four people are the driving force behind OpenCape. They are passionate, dedicated, persistent, and have contributed a lot of time to the project.

Integrated Community Representatives. The broader OpenCape Board of Directors represents the region geographically and functionally. They provide perspective and insight, connections to broader stakeholder communities, and can deliver on information or production needs when asked.

Government Contributing Supporters. Local, regional, state and federal legislators and administrators are an essential component of support. They can assist broadly in definition of need and development of solutions, and more practically in issues such as right of way access, regulation and resource development.

Non-Government Contributing Supporters. The broad economic goals of the region were essential to the development of OpenCape through such organizations as the Cape Cod Chamber of Commerce, the Cape Cod Technology Council, the Cape Cod Commission, and other entities.

Gallagher says all of this began with a summit in 2006 asking any one who thought broadband was an issue to join us to discuss solution, which about 100 people attended, and from there they took action to develop lists and a steering committee. People saw they we were serious and moving forward, so they wanted to be a part of that. Public awareness solved the issue of getting enough volunteers. A shared sense of community, even across municipalities with individual needs, keeps everyone actively engaged.

All of the members of the group have real jobs and do this work in their spare time. "Their motivation is the public interest, though it is also very helpful that most work for employers that will directly benefit from the project and therefore are afforded some flexibility of time," remarks Gallagher. "No project of this type will succeed without true believers willing to devote a considerable amount of their lives to its success."

Getting the best from your project team and steering committee

Mike O'Connor served on the Minnesota Broadband Task Force in 2009 as well as participating on several task forces previously involving large-scale technology issues. "Before you start to recruit stakeholders," O'Connor advises, "write a project charter, a project plan and a "sales brochure" that you use to go sell those stakeholders on why they should be part of your project. With these in place, you know who you have to recruit and why, you have a guide to help people better understand what they're signing up for and what's expected of them."

If you're going to set up a steering committee of stakeholders, choose them to be representative of the various constituent groups in the community. It's helpful if they have strong ties within their respective constituencies. The committee as a body should reflect the economic, ethnic, political and other aspect of your community's diversity.

Committee members need specific goals and established areas of responsibilities. One of those should be to play an active role in targeting and recruiting constituents to participate in the needs assessment. Make sure they target constituents for this process who have broadband access as well as those who do not so you are assured of getting a balanced picture of your needs.

The project team should be balanced according to individuals' skill sets and interests. For example, you need creative minds and detail oriented worker bees. A person very concerned about healthcare issues is an asset in a community where this is a big concern, and this person should be balanced with someone interested primarily in small business development if economic development is a major broadband objective.

Not everyone on the steering committee or the project team have to come to the group knowing a lot about broadband or technology in general. It helps, however, if they have a capacity to quickly pick up the basics of how a technology can be applied to meet average business or community needs. Conversely, your team or committee members who are the tech experts should have at least average people skills and ability to empathize with those who have zero understanding of technology.

The project team and particularly the steering committee should be run following the rules of good general project management. Work to ensure all the members learn the basics of operating with milestones, time frames and some sort of paper trail for their communications, including verbal. Anytime you have politics involved there are a greater number of people who you must communicate with and get to buy into broadband.

Keep everyone in both groups focused on what the end goals are. Keep everyone else in the community aware of what the project's successes are as they happen. There are likely to be many bumps in the road before you complete your broadband project. A focused project team and steering committee will adapt and perform to get past the bumps, while a constituency that sees progress most likely will continue to support you through these rough patches.

Characteristics of Good Team Players

The mayor, county commissioner, city council or other political leaders probably won't play an active roll in managing the project team's daily operations. But civic leaders can establish how constituents view your project. Having these leaders as proactive, publicly visible supporters of the project creates a buzz that increases your pool of qualified and motivated people to serve on your team. Those in the community who are good leaders and those who get things done want to play on a winning team. So early on be sure your political leaders publicly put the positive face of a winner on your broadband project.

The project leader

The person tasked with leading the project team and/or steering committee should be more than just a technologist or just a politico. The political climate around community broadband requires someone who is deft at handling occasionally clashing interests and personalities, and the technology is changing too quickly for someone who doesn't have at least a solid grasps of the key aspects of broadband. Of course, if you can't find a techie with political savvy, lean towards political savvy and good business sense. An IT staff person or competent consultant can compensate for a lack of tech expertise.

Additional qualities you want to look for in the leadership role is vision, the ability get others to share the vision, tenacity, multi-tasking capability, the ability to motivate volunteers and juggling skills. A sense of humor and appreciation for the absurd helps too. Other helpful traits include being knowledgeable about how organizations work, and the ability to create a positive group dynamic that fosters collaboration.

Richard Miller, VP of Marketing and Communications at Innovation Philadelphia, a consulting group that recruits technology companies to move to Philly, says you need to look for a "rainmaker" to lead your team. "This is the person who may not be the most detail oriented, but they know how to look at something, determine what the next phase is that needs to be done and make it happen."

The person leading your project doesn't necessarily have to come from within the government structure. Smaller government organizations may not have enough people with this skill set that you can afford to divert from other responsibilities. Miller suggests your team leader "could be an entrepreneur. When Innovation Philadelphia makes investments in projects, our investments are made with serial entrepreneurs who are strong in a specific discipline, and maybe this is their second or third company. You need people with that sort of entrepreneurial passion."

The project manager

The project manager needs to be strong in business or project management skills and have some expertise in technology deployments, even if it isn't broadband, because success or failure really depends on how well you manage the many details. Ms. Robinson has the tech expertise plus an MBA. There is a growing trend in some industries, hospitals for one, toward having the person who is driving their broadband implementation not be an IT person, but someone with business management expertise in that industry. CEOs believe this ensures the applications that get built will be more in line with the organization's business needs.

Your project manager handles all of the daily pieces of the implementation, including selecting the vendors and overseeing the physical infrastructure's buildout. Once the project starts generating publicity, constituents start asking "how can I join? Is there a benefit to my organization if we become part of this project? The project manager has to deal with these too. It's a continuous juggling act.

A good project manager who understands basic technology is usually capable of managing the broadband deployment, or buildout, phase because the technology requirements are relatively easy to grasp. You'll likely have ISPs, systems integrators, vendors or consultants available to help resolve the complex technology issues. But for pre-deployment there is a unique mix of business research and planning, economic strategy development, and policy development. There's also stakeholder analysis, planning responses to potential opposition, determining level playing field issues and working with a broad range of constituent groups. These require some level of business management skills.

Effective communication skills come in handy. Good negotiating skills also help, as the stimulus program encourages the creation of a sizeable number consortia comprised of multiple counties and stakeholder partners, some who may not have a great history of working amicably together . The team leader and the project manager both must be committed to delegating decision-making and other responsibilities to the various people and groups with which they work. "If you're bringing broadband access into a community that's never had it, you need to be sensitive to their social or cultural issues, and also to their feelings about technology," observes Miller. "Many people distrust technology given that it's new and outside of individuals' comfort zones."

Industry consultants are valuable team members

Whether your planned broadband coverage area is small or large, you may also find that a consultant becomes a third member of the project team leadership. This person may not be a pure technology consultant, but a blend of that and a government or general process management expert. These consultants and firms know the right questions you need to ask, players in the broadband industry and which technology trends require attention.

Fred Dyste, founder of Dyste Business Development, is helping Grover Beach, CA with a broadband middle mile project. "Often I consult as the project manager. Many clients do not lack employees or talent, they lack an available person with project management experience to bring the pieces together and see the project through to completion. A consultant saves them from the process of hiring a full time employee or overburdening an employee with additional priorities and responsibilities."

Dyste points out an effective tactic to help mitigate some of the "I don't work for you attitude" that employees can have with consultants. "'Peer' the consultant with an appropriate level executive or manager so that the consultant carries the authority of that manager with the members of the team."

Robinson feels that, "to find the right consultant, look very closely at their background working with communities and private sector organizations and see what they bring to the table." There's no rule that says you have to leave town to find the right consultant. In really small communities there still could be a number of homegrown sources of experts who like and play with this technology, such as universities. Broadband plays such a crucial role for communities you don't want to shortchange yourself, either. Cast the net near and far if the local talent pool doesn't cut it for you.

How do you know if the person sitting in front of you for an interview is really qualified? There are a lot of associations and industry groups that you can look to for input. The Internet itself is great place to go and research. Also ask around to other communities that have at least completed their broadband plans. If they used consultants they've likely had enough experience to give you a good critique of their consultants' positive and negative points.

Try to find consultants who have experience with cities or counties similar to yours. Deployments can be radically different from one place to another, so you need someone who understands the dynamics and type of technology, political and business challenges you face. Even the landscape is a factor. Someone who's only worked on fiber network deployments in the Southwest may be like a fish out of water when it comes to dealing with weather and soil issues in New England.

Once you bring a consultant on board, take effective action to ensure their success. "Establish clear cut and measurable objectives, advises Dyste. "Agree to a set number of hours or a 'per task' fee–which helps both parties stay within budgets and expectations. Keep the consultant in the loop. Don't omit them from informational e-mails and updates." Dyste believes consultants have some responsibilities in this relationship as well. "Try to be involved early in the planning process and when you are, listen, ask questions, and learn. Stay informed of the direction planning is going even if you are not tasked with all elements of the project."

The steering committee

Recruit people for the steering committee from the main constituencies you expect your broadband deployment to serve. Their input will be invaluable at aligning the technology with local business and community needs. It's important to select people who are used to rolling their sleeves up and getting work done. Philly's Executive Committee was able to do extensive qualitative research and write a business plan in just over 90 days while pilot projects were also being planned and launched. You don't get this kind of swift action from people looking to pad their civic resumes.

Neff brought the whole group together at the beginning of September in 2004, set the objective for writing the plan, defined everyone's roles, and specified the deliverables. Everyone on the committee worked on the plan, with small groups assigned to particular sections and everyone contributing to revisions of the final document. Before people left a meeting, it was clear that they had to deliver what they promised.

When the Mayor approached the individuals to participate on the committee, many were not aware of the idea except a few who might have heard a brief mention in a magazine or news article. Their reactions to the concept of municipal broadband varied.

President of Talon Solutions and consultant for companies managing large construction projects, Robert Bright recalls that "first I had a sense of curiosity. At the time, I was familiar with the technology. I knew you could have basic wireless at the house but I wasn't familiar with all of its potential uses. What does it mean, municipal wireless? It isn't until you get into it and understand some of the uses and benefits of broadband that you realize this is just the next step in Internet technology. There's not anything really new to it. You have electricity, gas and this is the next utility.

For steering committee member Pat Renzulli, former CIO of the School District of Philadelphia, the birth of Wireless Philadelphia coincided with an effort the school district already had begun. The District had its own robust wireless network development underway through e-Rate, a federal government program that provides funding for districts and libraries to build data and communication network infrastructure.

"The District did not see ourselves as a direct beneficiary of the Philly project, though we did explore the possibility of the city taking advantage of what schools had done," says Renzulli. "However, restraints on the funding prevented that option. On the other hand, we saw parents as being next logical group to benefit from online courses. Wireless Philadelphia can be that last technology mile to the parents."

One major benefit to creating such a diverse group and including people with little initial of understanding of broadband is that you significantly increase your odds of getting a plan that meets the greatest needs of the most citizens. Your main constituencies are brought into the process early so their needs and the unique opportunities that broadband off ers them are factored into the plan in a more objective manner. Also, these participants can start building foundations of support among these constituents you will need later. The people involved in the process who are learning about broadband are likely to spot potential flaws in the thinking of those who may be enamored with it, as well as broaden the team's thinking since their creativity isn't impeded by preconceived ideas.

As diverse as the group is and with the skill level that each member brings, the question comes up, how do you motivate these people who volunteer (meaning no pay) for jobs that could tests the limits of their professional skills? O'Connor believes it's "recognition, recognition, recognition. Sing the praises of those folks far and wide. Trumpet their early successes. Keep them in the spotlight whenever there's an excuse to do it. Help them build the network of friendship and trust within the task force. Recognition and support are the only coin you have available. Spend it liberally."

Project Teams at the Community Level

Your community has to determine whether you need to have pilot projects and how many make sense based on local factors. The number is likely to vary everywhere. What seems to be the norm in these constituent-driven projects is the collaborative team approach. In Philly there are constituent organizations such as the Greater Philadelphia Tourism Marketing Corp (GPTMC) and community services groups such as Lutheran Children and Family Services. These organizations partnered with leaders or other groups within their respective constituencies. Various vendors that were interested in bidding for the main deployment project, such as HP, Cisco, BelAir Networks and Lucent Technology, joined each project's partnership since the pilot was a good way to strut their technology stuff.

In a couple of cases, there were neighborhood-specific community services groups such as The People's Emergency Center in West Philly, or a larger organization such as the Philadelphia School District which already had wireless initiatives underway. In these situations, the primary task for Robinson was to bring these existing project teams into the city's efforts. There are probably as many ways to structure and populate a constituent-driven project team as there are constituencies and neighborhoods. But here are approaches that some of the groups in Philadelphia used.

Brian Loebig is the VP of Training and Quality Services for the citywide Lutheran Family and Children's Center. He played a key roll in the pilot in the Olney section. Loebig states that one of the things most critical to the success of a project such as this is the collaboration between the community and public and private sector organizations. Tech Access PA, which provides refurbished computers to people in need, Children's Network Service, Lucent, Ninth Wave Media, which developed the community portal and BelAir Networks all participated in this.

"We got a grant from the Lucent Foundation for $4,000 to help roll out the program. Since sections inside St. Paul's Lutheran Church [command central for the pilot launch] can't get good WiFi access because of stone walls, we also got a bridge to put in the bell tower that boosted the signal. Lucent's point person convened meetings with people in the community and also brought in people from one of the services agency to help with getting the word out. Our Executive Director and the Director of Church and Community Partnerships were active members of the group as well."

Keep Expectations Reasonable

With any project team, regardless of its focus, it cannot be stressed enough how important it is to manage expectations at all levels–politicians, employees, constituents, the media. If you look at why some teams are very successful with their projects and others have a very rocky journey or outright failure, how well they manage expectations is definitely a determining factor.

A classic example is when you have senior managers and elected representatives whose technology expertise comes primarily from James Bond movies, reading ads and listening to their newfound business flight friends. These people often expect more than a particular technology is capable of delivering. Reign in those expectations or these folks will be disappointed with the pilot results and want to kill deployment plans. At the very least, they will make it very difficult for you to get budget approval and move forward. Better to under-promise and over-deliver.

Managing the media relations effort well from day-one is critical to managing expectations. In media relations and all forms of internal and external communication, make sure everyone participating in the project and championing stay on the same page. Be very specific early on about what the tangible and intangible objectives are, technology capabilities, which mobile devices will be used, project timelines and costs, the potential benefits. Put these in writing, and have all the main stakeholders signoff (literally) on the document.

Any unexpected changes to the project that will significantly alter what people are expecting to see or achieve should be documented and distributed to the appropriate audiences. Making changes or adding new features mid-project will increase time and costs, and may even dilute the impact of the network. Be sure every stakeholder and partner involved clearly understands (also in writing) what their new expectations should be if they accept these changes.

While you want to manage as well what people on the project team expect, don't limit their flow of creative ideas or stifle their flexibility in dealing with the unpredictable changes, challenges or opportunities that pop up. This can cripple your ability to implement the best possible application. Make sure everyone is aware of the consequences of people's decisions so there are few surprises later.

To Sum It Up—A Project Team Checklist

Here are some guidelines to keep everyone on the same page.

1. Establish systems that allow team members, the steering committee and other stakeholder representatives to share ideas and track progress during the project to prevent a lot of duplicated effort.

2. If people outside of the project team will share data that sits on your current network servers, make the necessary technology and security provisions to manage their access. Establish secure accounts and authorization levels for everyone and be sure they fully understand what can and can't be done.

3. When hiring people and recruiting volunteers, consider not only each person's talent, but also the personal chemistry between key members of the team. Either resolve early what appear to be clashes that can harm the project, or re-assign people to different tasks or other parts of the team. You can't keep people on the same page if they don't forge a good working relationship with each other.

4. Establish procedures for rapid responses to really important questions, and timely quick responses to most of the rest.

5. Put a system in place to immediately cancel user access and passwords for those who no longer work on the project. Even though you're not working on top secret plans to invade the moon, there are times when some news and developments you'll prefer to keep "in the family."

Now, let's move on to the discussion on consensus building. If you don't do this part of the project well, there will be serious wailing and gnashing of teeth to contend with sooner or later. Probably sooner.

CHAPTER 5

Getting to Consensus—Not for the Faint of Heart

Consensus building is something you need to plan for from the first moment you broach the subject of broadband. There likely are some rough moments ahead. The larger the municipality or county, the more constituent groups there are with different needs and agendas. The topics around which you must build consensus can shift between this month and next.

A great deal of the success of your consensus building efforts rests on the skills of the person driving the effort to build bridges, form alliances and continually broaden the circle of believers. The rest depends on the project team and steering committee members each being a leader in their own right, carrying consistent messages to their constituents and constantly working the crowds (figuratively and sometimes literally).

This chapter gives you some helpful guidelines on getting your various stakeholders on board and in sync with the broadband effort, reaching out to diverse constituent groups, responding to some of the political challenges you may face. Even though it all looks daunting, it's still manageable. I cite many recent examples of consensus building, but I also reference Philadelphia's 2004 effort quite a bit because they offer some valuable lessons since they built consensus among many people for whom broadband was a foreign concept.

What You Say and How You Say It Is Key

Here are several points and recommendations to help shape messages that rally people around a technology that's a little difficult for some of them to fully comprehend. There's always more you can do to ensure that your early stages of consensus building are successful, so the following is only a starter kit.

First, whatever you mission is, state it consistently. If your municipality is going to improve government operations first with broadband and then tackle social issues, be clear about it and why you're doing things this way. Forget lofty statements. You're not writing the next Declaration of Independence. Rely on simple and to the point, such as "We're going to use wireless broadband to create a more efficient, responsive government." Clarity breeds consensus. Think: 30 seconds

Second, once you know what business model makes sense, put the word out on the street. Since this is where roadblocks to consensus building can pop up, you don't want to do a lot of waffling. If you have no intention of going into the broadband service business, state it starting today. If you plan to create a government/business partnership to offer broadband access services in which the city or county facilitate infrastructure access and service providers handle all of the business logistics of selling and supporting the service, lay it out there. Haven't decided yet which business model makes sense until you talk to constituents? Then that's your public statement. The clearer you are on these details, the faster you build consensus. Keep this discussion focused so you minimize misconceptions.

Third, make sure you have the facts about your community that help you create a sense of local urgency to make this project work. The U.S. has dropped from 3rd to 15th in the world in terms of broadband adoption by citizens, and the quality of our broadband is way behind many other countries. State how this impacts your local business community that has to compete in a global economy, or prevents disadvantaged businesses from growing and opening new global markets to stay ahead of local competitors. Relate the national stats on illiteracy to the numbers in your community, and then explain how your broadband initiative can help reverse the trend.

Fourth, be prepared to help people understand how the economics, deployment logistics, technological capabilities, etc. of your project offer advantages over alternative (or lack of alternative) Internet access options for constituents. Tell them to check the fine print when they do a cost/benefit comparison with competitors. What will "special low prices" revert to after the promotional period ends? When companies advertise data speeds of between 1.5 Mbps and 3 Mbps a year, is that true speed or just a bait and switch? Pocketbook issues bring people together.

Fifth, find a tech expert who can talk about technology so people with low technology-comprehension skills understand. Have him or her write one-page overviews of the various components of broadband networks and the applications you plan to deploy. Constituents who are pretty smart and wholeheartedly support broadband conceptually nevertheless can be confused by the basics when they first learn about it. Without clarity when describing what broadband does, recruiting supporters is challenging as you reach out to constituents who need to make it work in their neighborhoods and conference rooms.

Creative, occasionally comical, but never condescending materials are the way to achieve that clarity. Johan Kroes, Senior IT Architect for a financial services company in South Africa called Sanlam, states that "a great part of my job is to explain in simple laymen's terms what a system can and can't do. Make little analogies–this application is like a 4 x 4 jeep. It's great for these tasks, but you can't race it in the Grand Prix. Or, this connection is like a water pipe in your sink. You can't force 1000 gallons of water through here quickly." Make sure the people speaking on the project's behalf avoid jargon and geek speak.

After shaping the messages to win people over to your corner, the hard work is executing the activities that rally the various individuals and organizations around the messages so they take action that builds the broad support you need to move forward.

Moving forward with Consensus Building

The main person to initiate and sustain the opening push to recruit supporters for the broadband initiative may not be the same person to head the steering committee or the project team. It could be anyone who has a vision plus an aptitude and interest in learning how wireless can benefit governments.

"It doesn't matter if that person is with the education system or economic development, but they have to be someone the community can trust," states Don Speer, Executive Director of the Pulaski-Giles County Economic Development Council and main driving force behind the City of Pulaski's fiber network. "I remember in '94 talking to people about what was going to happen with Internet access when we were just trying to get dial up. Something like this has never been done before, and people looked at me like I was crazy." Speer was relentless and his message was consistent, so people in the community gradually got behind the project.

This lead champion also should be committed to doing a lot of legwork researching general broadband technology and specific potential uses of it for the city so he or she can make a credible case and turn everything over to the eventual project leader. They also should accumulate basic financial data about what these technology options may cost as well as what benefits the community and its stakeholders can reap from the implementation.

This preliminary work doesn't have to be a formalized process, nor does someone need to be "officially" recognized to pursue this task. In plenty of organizations it's the lone wolf working in stealth mode who does the work and when they feel they're ready, takes the idea to the powers that be. The first pitch for consensus should go to the most senior manager or elected official who can give the project legs and political support to sustain the effort once it picks up momentum. It may be useful to gather a little informal feedback from constituents before this meeting. Talk to two or three community players to see what they think about these ideas.

Building consensus at the highest levels

Technology initiatives in some organizations fall short of their potential benefits because top executives lack of vision and can't (won't) provide direction. Without enthusiastic buy-in and consensus on broadband at this level, successes will be limited and communities won't reap the full potential that broadband offers. Conversely, many of the broadband networks producing impressive results are doing so specifically because they have that top-level support within the key stakeholder organizations.

The operational structure of government varies by municipality and county. But regardless of whether you have a strong city manager, a strong mayor, part-time county commissioners or appointed people running the day-to-day operations, you have to get public support for broadband from the main public official who makes things happen. This person in turn can play a pivotal role in bringing other stakeholders onto the project team and steering committee. Know where the power lies and cultivate it.

Whether it's local government or your other stakeholder organizations, getting top-level buy-in is easier when the top dogs are committed to personally using the technology. Philadelphia's mayor in 2004 was a self-acknowledged gadget freak who carried a couple of different devices with him everywhere. He was that city's biggest cheerleader and instrumental in moving their wireless project forward. In commercial as well as government operations, part of IT's strategy for getting senior-level support for a technology project includes making sure all of the top executives get their hands on the technology. Try to use this tactic for broadband.

Early leadership can take many shapes

In many small towns and some cities the mayor may be the major catalyst. Or the mayor together with two or three other people could drive the process from the start. Within county governments, the person driving the consensus-building varies as much as the types of governing structures. Some counties have an administrator who operates similar to a city mayor, while others have Boards of Commissioners varying in size from three to more than 25 members. These could be elected or appointed officials.

Jeff Arnold, Deputy Director of Legislative Affairs for the National Association of Counties and a member of its Telecommunications and Technology Committee, believes there needs to be someone assertive who commands a lot of respect taking the activist leadership role. However, who will start the ball rolling is uncertain.

"I think what ends up happening is that the community actually starts the process. A citizen or group of citizens insists that 'we need broadband.' Either that county's administrator or a member of the Board of Commissioners has to step up to the plate and reiterate this is something we really want. It's all about someone understanding broadband and what it could mean, and being able to articulate this in specific terms. It's one thing to say 'broadband.' But what does that really mean? Is it WiFi, is it fiber? And what happens if people don't have it? If people haven't experienced it, how do you get them to understand what it can mean from a business standpoint as well as a personal one?"

As for stakeholder organizations such as hospitals, the school district or the chamber of commerce, the general dynamics of recruiting a champion to build consensus among their respective constituents are the same as with government organizations. Someone at or near the top of the organization has to see the benefit of broadband for their organization specifically and for their constituents. The leadership may go out to do consensus building, or designate some staff to do it. In the ideal situation, both the top brass and designated staff are getting constituents on the same page.

Building Consensus Within the Project Team

On the face of it, getting your project team on the same page is a straightforward proposition. You bring them in the room, spend some time explaining the vision, assure yourself that they're buying into the vision, give them their marching orders and away everyone goes.

Philadelphia's former Mayor Street and CIO Dianah Neff did great work getting the Executive Committee on the same page. The Mayor took care of the first round when he recruited everyone. He and Neff had worked out the mission statement, so each member joined the committee because they believed in the mission.

Neff then got the 17 members to come to consensus on a business plan that defined a network about which there were many unknowns, and created a business model for which there weren't clear precedents. This plan had to be clearly articulated so she could then build consensus around it within the various constituent groups. The committee as a body wouldn't be there to help since they were disbanded after presenting the plan to Mayor Street.

If the communities your network serves have diverse constituent groups with varying and sometimes competing needs, interests and goals, the project team or steering committee by default needs to be similarly diverse. This is the best way to bring the perspectives and feedback to the table to ensure that what you propose to your citizens are the tech solutions that they will support. With this diversity on the committee, however, you add more layers of difficulty getting everyone to support a document as complex as a business plan.

Veronica Wentz, Web Site and New Media Director for the Greater Philadelphia Tourism Marketing Corp. and member of the Executive Committee, states that "everybody was coming from a different place, and not everyone had the same level of understanding about the technology initially. Dianah did a good job of educating the group on what wireless broadband was about and what it can do. Then she asked people to bring back ideas on how they thought the technology could be applied in their business or community."

It helped a great deal that the People's Emergency Center (PEC) had a community WiFi project up and running that was brought into the Wireless Philadelphia series of pilot projects because Neff was able to use this to make the mission real. Wentz continues, "she always presented things to us to show how the technology had already made a big difference in some people's lives. 'PEC helps people better integrate into society. They refurbish old computers and have people up and running on the Net. This woman who was handicapped and had kids was able to start a business in her home and she pays $5 a month for wireless service.'"

Neff gave very good examples of how, in a small and focused way, this technology was being used. It was really easy to gain support around this. She kept everyone focused on the vision and the mission.

You don't need a hammer, just good direction

Another factor contributing to getting this diverse group in sync was "the fact that the mayor had put out the charge, 'we're going to do this." Adds Pat Renzulli, then-CIO of the School Board of Philadelphia and also a Committee member. "It was more an issue of how we did it rather than if we did it. I don't recall that there were many contentious issues. From the outset there were a lot of interviews of constituencies. What these tended to do was increase the reasons why we wanted to launch this project."

Richard Miller of Innovation Philadelphia concurs. "The discussion level in the group was always collegial versus controversial which helped us be successful. The blend of the people made this work. We all donated a great deal of expertise from our various fields–marketing, financial, technical. People were visionary and we're used to executing. Our reality was, here's the project, here's the concept. Now, how do you go through the process and get it done? Who you need on the team are people driven by the passion that comes with being able to take concept and build that concept into a reality."

Feedback from focus groups, which ran concurrently with the business plan writing, gave the committee even greater determination to make broadband work. It also helped them write a plan with greater persuasive powers in uniting people beyond the committee behind the project.

Robinson observes that, "after learning more about what the community felt, Neff was able to bring these results into the discussion. She was able to say 'this is how it's being received,' 'this is how people see applying it,' giving us more proof the idea was good. You need to pick out key points that by default generate universal support and then push these forward to the team and then to the communities."

Fast forward to 2009. The Minnesota state legislature, similar to Mayor Street, created a task force to create a plan for ubiquitous broadband throughout the state. Almost two dozen individuals were recruited, representing the full range of political leanings and a combination of public, private and nonprofit interests. Retiree Mike O'Connor was something of an at-large delegate representing metropolitan constituents. Looking at the group in the beginning, he and others were pretty sure this was going to be a near-impossible group to bring to consensus.

After many months, the task force achieved the impossible and did come to consensus on several key issues, including broadband speed goals and a goal to make Minnesota #5 in the nation in broadband access. How do you achieve similar results? "Several things are important," states O'Connor. First and foremost, it helps tremendously if people know what consensus decision-making is and how it's done. There are rules, tips and techniques to do this that people in your group need to know, and they need to understand why it's important. [Link provided by O'Connor to help you in this effort—http://en.wikipedia.org/wiki/Consensus_decision-making]

"It's also important that at least a few member believe in consensus and will nudge the group toward it when the going gets tough as people start to backslide into the old habit of just voting and getting on with the meeting. It's imperative that the Chair be one of the 'nudgers.' Without the support of the person running the meetings, it's almost impossible to keep a consensus process going. We were extremely fortunate to have a very effective Chair in Rick King who pushed us over the rough spots."

There are some who may look at consensus as weakness or the path to compromising away the path to the best solution to a local broadband issue. I take the view, all things in moderation. Some points you have to stand firm on or everyone but a few lose. As Dan Gallagher from OpenCape states, "We seek out input from all directions, and we've used an iterative process to continuously improve the concept and broadband plan. However, we avoided the ultimate pitfall of trying to be all things to all people and remained focused on our goal of a middle mile system." This approach still adheres to the fact you have situations where everyone winning something is better than one side or the other winning nothing. What you need are creative minds to find solutions that give everyone most of what they want while getting to your ultimate goal.

Consensus Building Among Constituents

You should spend time meeting with a lot of constituent groups to get their initial buy-in, to recruit them to relay the vision to their peers and neighbors and to keep them updated. There is a significant risk here trying to establish the project team's vision while helping constituencies refine their respective visions of what broadband means to them. The grand objective must align with these divergent objectives or else the online content and applications you build for the network will fall short of their potential. For an implementation of technology as vital as broadband, many constituents won't give you a second chance to prove yourself if you don't get it right the first time. You can build it, but people don't have to come.

Wireless Philadelphia's planning masterstroke was its 20 focus groups, each one representing a key constituency that collectively gave fair representation to technical, business, service and neighborhood interests. Two subsequent town meetings pulled in a greater numbers of city residents to both learn and provide feedback. These events got the word out to the communities that something exciting was getting ready to sweep Philly. People may not have understood it fully, but they wanted to be at the station when this train came in. "You can really go by what Philadelphia did because Philly did a lot of things right," states Robert McNeil, Principal of the Ronin Group that facilitated the focus groups and town meetings.

After collecting information and insights, you can rely heavily on pilot projects to get constituents in high-profile neighborhoods actively using broadband so the rest of the community is more likely to support the initiative. Community leaders and others participating in focus groups can become the main drivers for census building within specific neighborhoods, among businesses, on college campuses and within the health care community.

Remember that your approach to consensus building must reflect your area and the particular aspects of its respective constituencies. Little towns and rural areas tend to be more homogenous than big cities, so you'll likely only have two or three main constituencies to address and subsequently a lot less work to do. The objectives that you try to get people to coalesce around can be very different than what you've read about so far. Do your consensus building early so you get this heavy lifting out of the way. By the time you complete your business plan, your community supporters should be fully on board.

Getting in the trenches for consensus

One of the vendors bidding on the initiative's RFP was Lucent Technology, so they offered to donate equipment for one of the pilots. In May their community liaison Karen Archer Perry went knocking on doors in the Olney community of North Philly on behalf of Wireless Philadelphia. Her objective was to start building collaborative projects with organizations such as the.

Brian Loebig, of the Lutheran Family and Children's Center, states that "our mission is to help people in need, which dovetails with Philadelphia's mission to get technology into the hands of people who need it. To be successful, the city needs to continue to form these types of partnerships. If community people understand the services that are available to them, it will help take them out of poverty. Our organization sees the Net as an important way to do this, and this wireless initiative as an extension of the Net's capability. But you also need to have residents in the neighborhood take ownership of the project so they don't view it as someone coming in to do it for them."

It is particularly important that you approach this process without a lot of preconceived notions. "In some other neighborhoods where a lot of the women stay at home, online Martha Stewart recipes might be the thing to have," observes Patricia DeCarlo, Executive Director of Philadelphia's Norris Square Civic Association. "But that would be in those neighborhood. There were initial thoughts from the City that people could sit in the park here in Norris Square with laptops, which is a very middle class yuppie thing to do. Our folks do not have little laptops that they can take to the park. As broadband becomes more real, people become more vocal about what they need to do to make it better. Listen to them. Otherwise you're just wasting people's time."

Business communities may require different tactics

As for the business community at large, there are differing opinions on how much you do to get them supporting of the initiative.

"Some say you need to do the same type of consensus building for businesses in an underprivileged area as you do in the general community, but I think it's a little bit different," says Robert Bright, a business owner who was appointed to Digital Impact Group's Board of Directors. "Would it be nice to tell businesses, over there is such and such?' Sure, it would be helpful if someone shows you some things, such as 'these are the benefits of broadband, this is what it means.' It's also possible, as a business owner, to learn some things on your own doing research."

There are obvious marketing tactics you can execute to educate your business community about broadband so you get their buy in. However, business owners also need to understand their customers. If they're moving to broadband then business owners need to go that way. Robert continues, "When my clients say 'we're going to make all payments electronically now,' then I'm going to have to figure out how to do business like that. So there has to be some level of owner responsibility depending on whether or not you're serious about your business."

An opposite viewpoint comes from those who work in organizations and agencies focused exclusively to the economic development and improvement of their communities. They believe broadband will create additional jobs, enable businesses to expand nationally and globally through the use of the technology, and make their communities more competitive markets in which to do business. Such broadband champions typically advocate for aggressive marketing to ensure broadband adoption by businesses. I believe getting from here to there requires both external forces promoting adoption, and business owners willing to maximize broadband.

How aggressively you build support from commercial interests depends on how vested the project team is in your economic development effort, whether the discussion is just about businesses in blighted areas or the entire business community. I support a more aggressive approach to get their support early in the planning process. For one thing, this constituent group is where a lot of money, and therefore political clout, rests. It's easier to keep political opponents to community broadband at bay at the city and state legislative levels when you have strong business community support.

More importantly, business broadband subscribers are one of the keys to financial success of the network. Along with governments, strong commercial participation forms the foundation for sustainability. Once businesses become subscribers, they're customers for life as long as you provide great speed and great customer service. Your strategy for building consensus is to focus on this central group and its relationship to the community's economic development. It gets local business owners pumped up to be viewed as leaders in a cause that has such significance. They buy in and they actively work bringing in other businesses as customers.

General guidelines for constituent consensus building

From City Hall to the pool hall, until you know what people want, don't try telling them what they need. That's not consensus building. Let them tell you what they need or want. Focus your public proclamations on key milestones as you reach them, and relate these milestones back to addressing the input you initially received from constituents.

Make sure you have a good system in place to quickly identify, recruit and mobilize neighborhood and business champions for the project. Assign people to where they are needed most. The bigger the municipality or county and the greater the challenge, the more champions you need out there bringing the various constituencies into the cause. When all is said and done, as the network is finally deployed, generating communitywide broadband adoption is going to be a neighborhood-by-neighborhood effort.

The biggest threat to the success of community relations campaigns supporting broadband is inaction. Some people will talk or study an issue to death. At some point all of the various decision makers have to shut up and push the "Start" button on building public support. There's never going to be the perfect technology, political climate, business environment or product price.

Where the rubber meets the road…

From her experiences working with Philadelphia's project, Karen Archer Perry has distilled several guidelines for maximizing your efforts at building consensus at the constituent level. She is now working with the FCC on the national broadband plan.

Meet people one-on-one. The first step in community engagement is actually to engage people one-on-one and in small groups to tell them about the upcoming service, answer their questions and to solicit details about their needs and the needs of their clients and neighbors. People's ability to get over the technology hurdle and adopt something new requires a personalized view of what they need and how it will help them.

Clearly written collateral material is a must. Pay close attention to creating well-designed Frequently Asked Questions (FAQ's) pieces, brochures, maps of potential service areas, and other information that will allow people to understand how they will access the network. If people read good information that's localized for their community, their interest level and support for the initiative will increase significantly.

Broadband is not a one-size-fits-all offer. What people want to do with the technology dictates everything from end user and customer premise equipment that boosts wireless access coverage to what customers are willing to pay for it. You as well as the vendors and service providers you partner with must know and be able to explain what technology options best fit customers' particular needs.

Identify early adopters. Nothing sells better than a local reference. Use initial constituent meetings to identify early adopters who see the value in broadband and who want to champion the project widely in their community. They are the ambassadors for broadband. Look for diversity in initial contacts: people from area businesses, church groups, and different cultural groups that will share their enthusiasm with neighbors and associates.

Make the network tangible with launch events or demonstrations. If you are not already surfing at high speed, it's difficult to imagine what it means to have the world of information at your fingertips over the airwaves. Design a demonstration or launch event that showcases both the technology and the content. These must go beyond answering questions about technology, service and pricing. Constituents must get hands-on learning experiences to see what is available to those seeking information, services, education and entertainment, and the speed at which it will be accessible.

Plan mini events. While a large launch event or demonstration is a great way to introduce the new service, small activities are good for on-going efforts to reach people and build support. Consider attending chamber of commerce meetings, back-to-school nights, community meetings or even doing something on a street corner that shows off broadband service as the network buildout progresses. This is possible even if the service is running from a local store or café hot spot while you build out a proof-of-concept or pilot network.

Capitalize on interest with a local portal. If you have the resources, create a basic community Web portal that links to neighborhood and business groups, and includes local news or events. This enables people to get a more personalized feel for what broadband means to them.

Stay connected. Circle back occasionally and check in with these constituents during the build-out process, particularly the early adopters. Continue to share information with them as well as learn from them how to improve your plans and reach more people.

Building Political Consensus

The likelihood of facing political obstacles differs depending on where you are and what type of network business model you use. In some cases you won't be able to get telecos interested in bringing broadband to your area, but they become an obstruction problem as soon as others want to do it. In some cases, they'll fight you in the state legislature, but as we saw November 2009 in Longmont, CO, the incumbents also will fight savagely against municipal broadband at the city level. Comcast spent hundreds of thousands of dollars to kill an initiative to allow Longmont to study the possibility of making broadband services available to citizens.

The broadband stimulus program has been instrumental in bringing public-private partnerships front and center. In these arrangements, municipal or county governments are driving the project while private sector companies build the networks and manage operations. Other proposals have public utilities running the networks. As it became apparent that $7 billion is only going to fund a fraction of the communities that need broadband, many towns, smaller cities and counties have decided to pursue broadband on their own with the government driving the show. This drives incumbents crazy (networks totally run by private sector companies avoid some of this wrath, but not the anti-competitive tactics), and their reaction almost always involves attacks through the political system.

How are you going to educate your elected officials and representatives on the benefit of the technology? As I stated at the beginning of this chapter, whether you have a strong mayor, a strong council or county commissioners, you have to work closely with them to get them on board because their support is critical to overcome these political hurdles.

Achieving victory on the political battlefield

If you must do battle, understand that your two opponents likely are 1) the incumbents fighting what they fear as a critical threat to the weak spot of their business, and 2) a political philosophy that enshrines the concept of free market forces above almost everything else including community-run networks. These require different strategies.

The incumbents are a problem because fear makes conglomerates difficult to reason with and forces you into these life-or-death struggles such as we have seen in many states. Philosophically-driven politicians aren't much fun either, but at least cities have a philosophical counter punch that can be quite effective.

The strength of incumbents in their legislative counteroffensive to community broadband rests on money and knowledge since politicians always want money and never have time to learn all the details about everything they need to know. "We certainly see the 'money' factor," states Jeff Arnold. "The political reality is that incumbents that provision broadband have spent a lot of money with politicians in terms of campaign contributions. We saw that clearly in Pennsylvania in 2004. That's what the fuss was about. A whole lot of campaign contributions."

The money issue is why I often recommend that communities first deploy municipal broadband as a government business operations tool, and then build a strong support base of business people. A few thousand angry citizens can produce results, but sometimes it's easier for several mayors and county commissioners to rally a few dozen key business people to apply heavy pressure as needed. For some reason, there are legislators who seem to respond a little better to a phone call from a millionaire or two than calls from the average citizen. In the ideal world, having a vocal coalition of community activists and businesses laying on the pressure is best.

So, how do you rally the business community around broadband? Point to three hot-button issues.

Bringing businesses into the legislative fray…

Unless a company has the clout to whittle an exception from city council, most businesses pay local government taxes and fees. Point out that any smart business wants those tax dollars maximized to get the greatest efficiency in services that the government delivers. Everything from building inspections to paperwork processing and traffic control around their places of work can improve with municipal broadband.

Second, public safety issues are business issues. What would happen if business owners' plant, office buildings or homes suffered preventable losses because their city is hindered from improving its communication infrastructure and operating procedures? As hurricanes Katrina and Rita painfully illustrated, wireless text messaging might be the only communication lifeline business and employees have after a natural or other disaster hits.

Third, most responsible business managers would rather spend $25 or $35 per month for highspeed access for each mobile worker rather than $60–$80/month for slower speeds. Local governments driving partnerships in which a new breed of ISP leverages the latest technology to deliver a superior service at a better price gives businesses a better business technology option that directly impacts their bottom line.

Knowledge distribution is power

With technology-related bills, most local or national elected representatives who don't understand the features and business or social impact of the technology in question rely on someone else to give them that information. Typically, industry lobbyists are the ones who roll in the font of knowledge from which these politicos partake, which needless to say isn't going to paint a pretty picture for municipal broadband.

You need an education campaign specifically targeted to your representatives that not only presents key arguments in favor of broadband, but also delivers the same types of technology-made-simple documents recommended for use in your community relations efforts. Control the discussion and impact the bills written in your state by influencing what representatives learn about wireless. How you execute this education campaign is dictated by the local circumstances and personalities of your respective legislative bodies. But it is imperative for you to run such a campaign.

Even if your state legislature isn't threatening to prohibit community broadband, you have to worry about other laws that can adversely affect your initiative. For example, in Westchester County, NY several years ago, an effort took flight to pass a bill requiring Internet cafes and commercial businesses that use wireless networks to take basic security precautions to protect private customer information from potential data thieves and hackers. Fines would have been assessed for those that don't comply. Gauging from the resulting blogs written by tech-savvy people, the intent was commendable, but the approach that the county was trying to codify was flawed.

The way to minimize these potential minefields is to build a rapport early on between your project team and two or three representatives who are likely to be the main people driving technology bills within a particular body–city council, state legislature, etc. It's usually the person most knowledgeable about technology that other representatives rely on to determine how they vote. Having a "trusted advisor" relationship with these individuals keeps you in the loop so you can be proactive rather than reactive while enabling you to gain some level of counterbalance to lobbyists' activities. You want a seat at the table–or at least an ear at the door–when these late-night bills are being drafted.

Make no mistake, though. There are counties and states where the politicos driving anti muni broadband legislation are firmly in the pockets of incumbents who pay their campaign tabs. There are several towns and counties in North Carolina that have proven successes with community broadband networks. But no amount of education seems to prevent some of their state legislators from every few months introducing legislation to kill these networks. So go as far as you can trying to get people to see the light, but be prepared to fall back on rallying the masses and the business community to assert your desires through the election and legislative process.

When the opponent is philosophy

In the philosophical battle you have a political faction who say that local government should never be competing with the private sector. The incumbent telcos play this card a lot, though I believe they do this as a means to an end rather than from any adherence to political ideology. You need to bring out your trump card. Ken Fellman, former Mayor of Arvada, CO and current President of National Association of Telecommunications Officers and Advisors, spells it out this way.

"The state or Federal government shouldn't be telling local governments what to do. It's easy for us in local governments to argue this point and a difficult position for conservative legislators to argue against because, while they like to be pro-business, most conservative philosophy argues for local control. Whether it's a town of 500 people, or a city of millions, if citizens examine the issue and say 'we are willing to spend our tax dollars, we're willing to vote for a tax increase or issue bonds because we think municipal broadband is a good idea in our little town, then who are you at the state capitol to tell us we can't do that?' We thought you supported local control? Isn't that what you're party's all about? This argument resonates."

The decision to deploy municipal broadband is no different than when that same community decides they should issue a bond to build a new road or new baseball fields. Or they want to spend money for bigger pipes in their water system to get more capacity to address the increase in population. What legislature is going to tell a public utility they can't build a new electric power grid? Oh, wait, they did try that 100 years ago. Municipal broadband's the same deal. Since Colorado already has a law that says muni broadband services must be approved by local vote, Comcast's friends played on this "government shouldn't do it" philosophy with the Longmont electorate. Same crap, different shovel.

"In order to fight this battle, look for coalitions because this battle isn't all liberal Democrats versus conservative Republicans," Fellman states. "When you get into these debates, a lot of times it's the rural areas that aren't covered and they're the ones who will benefit the most, at least initially, by putting in a broadband system. A lot of those areas are represented by conservatives who may likely look at the debate and say, 'this isn't just business versus government, it's about local control.'"

One strong card in your hand is the broadband stimulus grants and the drive by the Obama administration to raise the national quality of our broadband. The National Telecommunications and Information Administration (NTIA), one of the agencies awarding grants, wants to "push people to be more creative and more inclusive" through public/private partnerships that "reach out to all the key anchors in a community." NTIA indicates that it plans to put its money where its mouth is, literally. Once other communities see these projects come to life, desire to keep up should trump philosophy for many constituents.

Arnold offers an additional tact to turn the gods of market forces in your favor. "In most cases, the citizens want what they want when they want it. People are beginning to understand broadband more and more. Broadband acceptance is moving quickly because anyone who's ever experienced it doesn't want to go back. There's an interest among those underserved communities to get any kind of broadband. If this is true in your county, discuss the market demand and show how municipal broadband makes sense because it's the cheapest and fastest alternative."

Once you build support based on market demand, you've elevated the discussion so people with different philosophies can come to the table and talk about how to get more broadband and more competition into your communities. In some cases that will be the government itself providing services, in others it will be the city seeking private sector partners. You may find that the government/business partnership option is what enables you to find middle ground with the private sector advocates, and you can move forward.

To Sum It Up

Consensus building is the lifeblood of a successful municipal broadband deployment. Plan on it, execute on it, insist on it. Fellman concludes, "I believe, and others I know believe, that good local leaders try to see the future and where everyone needs to go. Then we help people get there a little faster than they would if you weren't pushing them. If you're really good at it, you have people think they got there all by themselves."

CHAPTER 6

Understanding the Needs and the Will of "We the People"

Two things were evident as I researched details of Philadelphia's use of focus groups and town meetings for my last book. First, these were incredibly effective tools for building consensus because their impact went beyond helping the Executive Committee rethink some of its assumptions while formulating its business plan. Second, this was a better effort at understanding end user needs than even some major corporations with large budgets do when it comes to technology applications.

In this chapter I present an in-depth look at Wireless Philadelphia's focus groups and their impact on the planning process, and discuss the role they played beyond gathering feedback. This process is a standard for due diligence that communities should try to match or exceed to be sure that the broadband you ultimately deliver meets the desires and needs of We, the People.

The Philadelphia experience is also important because it embodies the role of local government in driving the needs assessment process. Regardless of who physically builds or owns the network, those living in the community are the customers, and if you don't know your customers, you can't make a product or service successful.

Paul Larsen, Economic Development Director for Brigham City, Utah, concurs. "The analysis needs to be driven by those with the greatest interest in the outcome and should include local elected and appointed officials, business owners, interested citizens, and technical experts. They are best qualified to determine what the community's needs and wants are. Much of what could be considered economic impact analysis was a result of the deep understanding of the community by those involved in the Box Elder [county] Telecommunication Partnership (BETP) and the Brigham City task force." Larsen is also a member of the Executive Board of Utah Telecommunication Open Infrastructure Agency (UTOPIA), a collective of 16 towns building its own fiber network.

Philadelphia's Atypical Efforts Produced Great Feedback

One shortcoming I've seen with technology deployments over the years is that organizations don't spend enough time listening to the people who actually use the technology. It's not necessarily a function of money. Companies with lots of money are just as guilty as cash strapped groups. Sometimes I gather it's the ego of the people driving the process and their assumption that they know best what users need. It's often the case that project managers are heavily time constrained because of so many other commitments. Regardless of the cause, the reality is the more end users you listen to, the better the application is that you design and deploy.

To pursue a grand vision of resolving social needs for a diverse population, spurring major economic development and making a town or city more desirable for visitors demands an aggressive needs assessment effort.

It is possible to do quantitative research in which you mail out lots of surveys and conduct numerous phone or on-the-street interviews. However, for complex products or concepts and new technology, you also need qualitative research where people in the process have time to get their minds around what you're talking about. Broadband definitely requires the latter research option. Larsen observes, "in my opinion, these kinds of analyses are as much subjective as objective. No analysis can precisely predict the response in the market to this kind of an undertaking. There is as much art as science in preparing and interpreting the analysis."

Philly sets itself up for success

In order for the Executive Committee to meet its aggressive three-month deadline for developing the business plan, they pursued several tasks in tandem. Area universities, including Temple, were contacted and student/professor teams were recruited to gather industry and financial data to help the committee make choices regarding technologies and business models. Community business leaders and representatives from the school district were contacted to assess their respective perspectives on municipal broadband. And the committee decided to use focus groups and town meetings to capture feedback from a broad spectrum of stakeholders.

To develop the focus group process, the committee brought in Julie Fesenmaier, Associate Research Director at the Cochran Research Center in Temple University's Fox School of Business and Management. The Ronin Group was chosen to facilitate the focus groups and the town meetings.

Focus groups are different than town meetings in that the focus groups have fewer participants, maybe 15–20, and are conducted as an intense roundtable discussion in a closed setting. Philly held 20 and each group was comprised of people from a particular stakeholder constituency. A city or county this size (1.5 million people, 135 square miles) should have anywhere from 20 to 30 sessions to make sure you get the broad representation that's needed if you want to an accurate picture of what your communities think. A town meeting is a larger gathering, participation is open to all communities, and each meeting may attract 50–60 people. While the discussion is still controlled, it is not as tight and intimate as a focus group.

An important milestone was to define who the stakeholders for the focus groups should be. The tendency is to just suggest technology users. But Fesenmaier strongly advocated for the Committee to hear from all the stakeholders, whether their comments were for, against or neutral. This included inviting the incumbents that weren't supporting this, though in the end they didn't share any opinions even after the committee tried to set up a focus group just for them. Julie says "if I hadn't pushed the committee on this, the quality and accuracy of the feedback would not have been nearly as good. They let me define who the stakeholders were going to be and what kind of questions we were going to ask them."

Identifying key issues…

Fesenmaier created a workbook for identifying key issues that the committee completed together in a session. It was a vision exercise in which everyone had to articulate what they saw as the best case scenario for the network and what was the worst case scenario. It's a random thought process to see what comes out. "All of these diverse people brought in from education, health care, general businesses and so on, had to buy into a multi-faceted definition of what this initiative meant. In the session they also had to list categories of stakeholders the focus groups would represent."

The workbook started with questions such as "What benefits does a wireless community bring to its residents?" and "What does that perfect wireless community have?" Some of the leading responses from members were "accessibility," that the network not be limited to time or place, that there be unlimited information, and "opportunities," the network has to offer equal access, business opportunities and education enhancement.

Members were asked to define the characteristics of a wireless community that has good services and infrastructure in place, and a wireless community with poor infrastructure. They cited cost effectiveness, reliability and security among the positive characteristics, and bad service, bad publicity and lack of user friendliness among the negatives.

The committee had to describe the main functions they saw the network serving in the community. Leading responses included "increasing connectivity between businesses and customers" and "improving the quality of living." There were also questions about how to ensure the sustainability of the network, to which some of the key factors were continuous funding and financial viability, partnerships and collaboration.

Finally, the committee worked through a list of 30 values in order to assess "What values drive the development of this community technology program?" Looking at each value, what's of great importance or less importance? The top values for the committee were being innovative, providing leadership, being reliable and being responsive. Julie wanted to be sure that these values were reflected in what the focus groups discussed. At the end of the session they developed a list of participants and questions for the focus groups.

Facilitating the focus groups

Though there are firms that coordinate all of the logistics of focus groups for a client, the committee decided to do things differently," states Ronin Group Principal Robert McNeil. "Various members of the committee had ideas and contacts for potential participants. We recommend that if a city is going to select participants, look at the stakeholders groups they know and get as broad an audience as possible of people who have an interest in wireless.

Committee members reached out to several colleges, hospitals and chambers of commerce. They went to individuals who represented large groups. They also did the cut economically, so members solicited different organizations and community groups within neighborhoods. This was easy for Philadelphia because it's a city of neighborhoods with very active associations such as the Asian American Chamber of Commerce. The committee also wanted people who didn't belong to an organization, but who were recognized members of particular communities so there would be representation of a geographical area rather than a particular group.

You can ensure diversity of opinion even within a group of seemingly similar people. Participants can be a from a group of colleges, so they're homogenous that way, but if they don't know each other then they're still diverse in terms of how they might have used broadband technology or may want to use it. You will get better information than if you bring in a fraternity group or some other group in which people know each other.

Running focus groups effectively

Needless to say, asking the right questions makes all the difference in the world to the outcome of the focus group process. Some of the committee's focused on pricing and how much would people pay. There were questions about what people thought the benefits were. A major question was, did participants think that the city should operate the network along the lines of a pubic utility, or should an independent consortium or a cable company run it?

A lot of energy went into the question design and refinement process that is atypical in standard focus groups. Fesenmaier and McNeil took the committee's questions, added their own, and then went back and forth many times refining questions until they had 25 they wanted to send to the committee for final approval. They had meetings after the initial focus groups to talk about the questions some more. "This question is getting flat, what do you think about changing it around?" About six didn't really produce that much information, so these were replaced.

The classic focus group format is to have people come in and you ask them a set number of questions, usually in sequence going around the room to get everyone's answer. But when you do it this way, people start influencing each other's answers and you don't get the type of candid responses as you might in other formats. McNeil's approach was to ask participants to write their responses first on index cards, and then get them to state their answers.

"This is a little bit longer, but we felt we got better information. If people work on something individually and then they talk about it in a group, they're more likely to state their own opinion than that of the person before them. By writing it down they formulate their opinion first." Another thing McNeil did to facilitate discussions was follow the energy in a meeting. "If it was getting hot about something, we could pursue that. For example, it got hot around the digital divide in a lot of sessions."

Another thing you want to do is control for over-speak so that you hear from everyone, not just the assertive people. McNeil intervened pretty quickly if someone started to dominate the discussion. "You want to create a 'protected' atmosphere to ensure that each person's opinions is fairly independent, which happens when you give people a sense of freedom of response and they feel like they can speak candidly."

Encouraging candidness is important if you want to maximize the main benefit of focus groups, which is to get quality of responses by delving deep into people's thinking. You get to ask follow up questions, or have interplay going across the group so someone can add to what someone else said. This way, you get a smart group that responds. You're not dumbing down the process by asking all the groups the same questions. Also, when people from diverse groups push along different paths, but come back with some similar conclusions, you know you're coming to some collective consensus that will help unite the general population.

Philly goes the extra mile to maximize benefits…

To get the most benefit from your focus groups, you have to have more than a passive involvement with their execution. Don't let things rest just with the facilitator. The committee received reports after each session and a videotape to review if they wanted to get a better sense of some of the emotions in the group, and members also were invited to participate in the sessions.

Those who attended were able to push the group even more than the facilitator, though he still maintained control and direction for the sessions. McNeil recalls a group of African American businesspeople in one session when the question came up about whether wireless would be useful for low-income residents and how. Participants were answering when someone from the committee said "you're not really addressing the question of will there be a digital divide if we bring in wireless and everyone can't access it."

A person in the focus group shot back, "where have you been? There already is one! Some of us have computers, some of us don't. Some of us don't even have a clue. The digital divide is all around. It's not that a question of are we going to increase it or decrease it, it's already here. If you're going to address it seriously, then you're also going to have to provide access to a lot of folks. Access might actually mean training, it might mean computers, or it could be some other kind of solution that you may not be thinking about." The committee got a lot more information at a level where they could feel the intensity of the disenfranchised people in Philadelphia.

Besides good feedback, you also want to convert focus group participants into broadband champions. What the committee did was to create the vision of a wireless Philadelphia and gave people an opportunity to contribute to the vision. What's more, they told participants that a small part of the network was already up and they could go to a section of city and try it out. "This is really important," McNeil says, "because it wasn't an abstract concept at that point. If anyone wanted to see how it would work they could go down by the LOVE statue across from City Hall and see it. A number of people had actually tried it before the focus groups."

It was also beneficial that Varinia Robinson and her group were quite savvy about making the focus groups a marketing force. The participants were movers and shakers, the connectors. They would go back to their constituents with brochures she created and say "look, this is what's happening. I was just in a focus group and these are the things we can do with wireless." McNeil asked participants to invite people to the town meetings. Participants were sales people as well as believers when they left the sessions.

Making participants feel special is another way to maximize the benefits of the sessions. One of the challenges running focus groups is making sure that people attend. A committee subgroup did a good job of providing an added personal touch. The staff contacted participants to make sure they were coming and had food in place when everyone arrived. Everything was top shelf. The sessions were invitation only. They were in nice rooms with great facilitator equipment. It was clear to attendees that the city was very serious about this from the very moment it started.

McNeil believes these little details "show that a city is welcoming, appreciative that people gave up time to make an important contribution and interested in what participants have to say whether you agree with their opinions or not. What was nice in Philly was that we had high-level doctors from prestigious hospitals and community leaders from some of the low-income sections of the city, and everyone was treated the same way. People felt a little special for giving their input."

Town Meetings Bring It All Home

Philadelphia has a history of town meetings. For example, if the regional public transportation system (SEPTA) is considering a fare increase, there's always a big town meeting about it. The city convenes these for many issues about which they want feedback. These two for municipal wireless were broadcasted on one of the local TV networks so people could watch and also link in via phone. "The dynamic that's different from focus groups is that you don't know who's going to show up," McNeil remarks. "Who usually shows up are the interested parties, of course, so we expected representatives from general communities, business people and the telcos." Well, two out of three isn't bad. The telecom and cable companies didn't show, or at least didn't make their presence known.

The meetings produced very engaging conversation going back and forth that flowed mostly on its own. McNeil just opened up the discussion and fielded questions so people felt there was an organized process. People asked questions and others gave strong opinions about what they thought. Both sessions were very favorable for broadband.

"From my experience with other town meetings, these two were well attended and we got a diverse audience," according to McNeil's critique. "I was expecting fewer people or more people that to be focused on one side of the discussion. We didn't have people who were advocating either for or against this. The meetings were more like information-gathering sessions. I was surprised because a number of people actually used it as a focus group and brain storming process. 'Well, if we do this, do you think we could use it for that other application?' There was the fellow speaking on behalf of seniors asking if they would have access helpful information about health conditions."

The entire Executive Committee was at both meetings getting into discussions directly with participants. Once you get so many people from all walks of life taking time from their schedules, volunteering ideas in a public forum, and building on each other's ideas, you're another big step closer to matching the right broadband technology to constituents' needs.

Though you can do either focus groups or the town meetings first, McNeil thinks it was good the way Philadelphia did it. "We became good at asking the right questions in focus groups, so we were really up on what the themes and major issues were. When we got to the town meetings I had a thorough understanding of what the Committee wanted to know, and it was rather simple to follow up on attendees' questions. When someone presents a question, it's good when the facilitator can ask 'well are you also talking about…' and probe what it is that people want to know. Since the Committee had the results of focus groups, they also were knowledgeable and better prepared for the town meetings."

Do you have a creation orientation?

The tone that you set for the focus groups has a lot of impact on what you get out of them. Philadelphia tapped into what McNeil calls a "creation orientation" instead of a "problem solving orientation." As a marketing person who's worked on both types of projects, I have to say that you really get more mileage with the former than the latter.

When you try to create something you bring something new into being, and there's a lot of energy you can get around "wouldn't it be cool if…?" brainstorming. You get this incredible vision out there with lots of people contributing to it because they can be a part of the dream. The problem solving orientation is typical when people deal with government. Instead of trying to bring something new into being, you're trying to make something go away. "Make my taxes go away." Make this or that problem go away." There's often not a lot of positive energy in these types of meetings.

"So we weren't trying to say 'what are all the problems we can expect with putting up wireless in Philadelphia,'" remarks McNeil. "Because of the creation orientation, there were many ideas bubbling up in all of the focus groups and town meetings. 'I can be sitting on the bus and contact a restaurant to make reservations for dinner using my handheld?' 'You mean I can use that thing to Google a company while I'm waiting in the lobby to meet with them?' People were building on each other's ideas. We were going to make this network come into being. And believe it, this is a vision. Yet it's concrete enough that people actually believe it can happen."

The committee was making plans for what they wanted and what they thought the people needed, yet sometimes they were surprised by the responses of the focus groups. They really needed to see up close and personal what it was that people were really interested in doing with the technology. They were able to come back from a focus group and say they had better insight to the emotional tone.

Knowing what people want and the emotional intensity of their need is important to the discussion about political consensus building. McNeil observes, "there were people who didn't think muni broadband was worth while at all. Even though they weren't in the majority in the focus groups, they were still there and they were very candid. Politicians need to see all of these viewpoints on the discussion because sometimes they are not in sync with what people feel."

Fesenmaier had a student go to all of the sessions to take notes on specific observations. Her and McNeil's reports were all pretty extensive. After reviewed the documents and some of the tapes, she wrote the final analysis report. It takes a fair amount of work after transcribing everything to make sense of what people said, and the researcher has to make sure that their personal leanings don't filter into the results. This is why the tapes are important.

"I feel pretty confident of the results," Fesenmaier concludes. "I believe that the users determined the way these focus group went and the results we got reflect people's true feelings. I would have like to have had the media there, but we didn't think about them until it was too late. The media comes in with different principles and values about broadband and I'm sure their opinions are not unanimous. And it could have been good to hear what the Comcasts had to say. I talked to some of them informally, but they just said "it's never going to go," and brushed everything off.

Broadband Mapping Adds Needed Dimension to Needs Assessment

If the focus-group/qualitative approach used by Philly and others represents the art of needs assessment, then broadband mapping is the science-oriented side of this task. Or it would if politics hadn't bastardized the underlying value of mapping.

The average person who's aware of broadband mapping through most news accounts likely assumes its primary purpose is to create a pretty map that shows you who has or doesn't have Internet access. This perspective is reinforced by media accounts of Senators protesting the fact the government budgeted $350 million to create these maps.

[My December 2009 Fierce Broadband column here throws light on what should be the true role of mapping if you want to maximize the benefits of needs assessment]

In general I find it difficult to get overly excited about criticism of a technology initiative from a particular Senator who has to rely on his wife to open his e-mail because he doesn't know how. Really. Say broadband he probably thinks "Dixie Chicks."

However, the Senator's recent criticism of the $350 million set aside for broadband mapping grant has some merit. Sort of. The problem isn't the money, though. It's the mission!

People in D.C. and across the nation assume the mission is to create state maps showing who has or doesn't have broadband, and roll these into one national Web-based map. It's not. The mission is–or should be–to execute an effective broadband needs analysis so the FCC can create an effective national broadband strategy plan. The difference is not a game in semantics.

Many people who've implemented high-priced, complex technology projects start with an extensive needs analysis that looks at current and future end user needs, technologies currently in place plus a dozen or so other factors and variables. To do anything less threatens the success of the project.

The new administration and Congress want a strategy plan for transforming how the U.S. (we the people and all our institutions) does business by significantly upgrading our broadband capabilities. Creating a good plan requires a thorough multi-faceted needs assessment. By giving away millions of dollars to just show who has and doesn't have broadband severely shortchanges the broadband needs assessment process both locally and nationally. The mission does not achieve the goal.

What we need to do is not complain about the money but educate the states to change the mission. Focus on doing comprehensive needs analysis. The map is simply the medium through which you represent the market intelligence the needs analysis collects.

Effective broadband strategy through better market intelligence

The FCC, bless 'em, is actually doing a lot of good needs assessment work already. Here's how the states can use that grant money to raise things to the next level.

First is the obvious work of gathering numbers on who doesn't have any broadband and where these individuals and organizations are located. It actually can be a painful and expensive exercise, but there are ways to make this less painful.

The second step is to pinpoint who has broadband and what type. Some folks don't place high value on this, saying we just need to focus on the have-not's because they're the only ones who need broadband. However, effective needs analysis requires a more comprehensive picture. To transform local businesses into international players and boost the local economy, you need to know what people have in order to clearly understand what they need.

Third, determine what changes are predicted to happen within specific industries, constituent groups, demographics, etc. that broadband can facilitate or remediate. Furthermore, what do constituents expect to do with broadband in three-to-five years? If our national strategy is to be effective, it must be forward looking.

Fourth, create an inventory of existing broadband resources: fiber lines owned by non-government organizations, towers, public hotspots, vertical assets that can support wireless infrastructure. Where are transportation or public works projects scheduled that you can leverage to install fiber conduits? What are the technology roadmaps and planned enhancements for current infrastructure that can boost broadband coverage?

The broadband map–not just another pretty face

An effective national broadband map is not, as some critics seem to believe, a one-dimensional snapshot of blue data points and red data points you get for free on Google. It's a dynamic visual representation of myriad data that enables you to show multi-dimensional "living" views of what your broadband strategy should be.

When the needs assessment is done properly, one map layer shows who has broadband speed sufficient for reaching a community's economic, educational or healthcare goals. A second layer shows you how to save money by tapping into broadband resources of particular constituent groups. Another estimates what coverage or speeds you'll need in two years based on projected changes in population, or what industries come to town.

Collect the right broadband data, combine if with census and city/county planning data and the map helps you refine broadband strategy to support cities of the future. With constituents' and institutions' data on predicted broadband usage, your otherwise simple map becomes a digital crystal ball. State or national broadband maps can become integrated features in animated Web-based community marketing content.

Integrate the right sets of data and you won't have to ask again, "hey, got a map for that?" Re-direct money from coercing usage data from incumbents and put it into building better networks. Plumb the depths of the Internet, directly poll the people who use the Net. Good systems automatically refresh maps with this new data, while data sets validate each other.

All of this begs the question, did we get it backwards waving money around enticing broadband proposals without knowing true broadband needs? Yes. But that train has long left the station, and the politics are such it ain't coming back. Fortunately, we can still save the day with a better end game than starting game.

Now's a good time to note that its aggressive use of workshops in DC and across the nation, plus actively gathering public comments, have done a reasonably decent job of needs assessment. If the FCC presents their strategy plan in March as a living document rather than the final word, they and others can use a strong guiding hand to move the states' mission from creating maps to executing effective needs analysis that collects strong market intelligence. The data and resulting maps can help the FCC and local communities refine their strategy plans.

Broadband mapping's role at the local level

My column may have given you the impression that only states will be developing broadband maps. That shouldn't be the case. All of the details I outlined that a typical statewide map should reflect can be captured at the county or city level. Benicia is a small community in California that released an RFP in 2009 for a needs assessment that has many of the mapping details my column proscribes.

Yes, it's true that states have money to conduct mapping tasks, but it's unclear how uniform these efforts will be from state to state. Ideally, the states should be using the money they've received plus possibly some of their own to help local communities contribute to the process. But your project team should determine how you can at least execute the surveys of consumers and businesses, assemble a technology inventory, anticipate future trends and so forth, even if you can't create a super sophisticated map to show the data. The knowledge. It's the knowledge you want to gather.

"Understanding current broadband usage by geography is an ongoing need for communities as well as for the broadband and wireless carrier community," states Adam Elliott president of data analytics company ID Insight. "By creating easy access to extensive data and sophisticated analytics, we see a phenomenal opportunity for service providers and communities to develop a data-driven approach to planning so they gain access to funding that may have otherwise been impossible to get. In the end communities will get better broadband."

The Role of RFIs (Requests for Information)

Bringing all of your constituents together to build creative energy and enthusiastic support for your municipal wireless initiative sets the stage for the important next step of the implementation process, matching the right technology with user needs.

Requests for Information (RFIs) are issued by organizations that understand their staffs don't have a lot of expertise in a particular technology and its use. RFIs are an open call to the technology industry in search of a number of experts who will come in to brief the staff in person, or just provide a written response, on the basics of the technology. The information and ideas that come from this process help the organization better understand its needs, more effectively assess its technology options and develop a better RFP. The logic is sound, but there are a couple of potential problems you want to avoid.

For one thing, you may be eliminating input from the vendors who can do you the most good if your RFI is too extensive. Many RFIs issued during the muni wireless craze were more than a request for a sitdown roundtable discussion and technology briefing, but closely resembled a full RFP in terms of the amount if information requested. However, responding to the RFI was no guarantee of winning a contract so a lot of vendors wouldn't bother to reply to them.

Do your own homework

These suggestions for the RFI process aren't about making life easier for vendors, they're about understanding whose role it is to do the homework necessary to determine–and be able to articulate to vendors–the needs of your citizens. This is how you best define what broadband should accomplish so vendors can give you valid ideas on what technology is best suited to your situation.

Butcher from Intel states that "vendors like it when the community has done all of its homework and has committed to focusing on one or two key applications. You need to have gathered feedback that answers venders' main questions. What are the priorities within the government and from their stakeholders? What do their citizens get from this? Vendors like the idea that a community has tracked where all of its network resources are, such as fiber in the ground. Local government needs to know if it has access to key assets such as lampposts and rooftops that are needed to deploy the infrastructure for wireless. All of this helps vendors design responses that are the most appropriate for you."

Ken Fellman, President of NATOA, describes details that went into the 2006 RFI issued by Colorado Wireless Communities, an intergovernmental agency of 10 municipalities, including Arvada, Colorado, where Fellman served as mayor. "Here's what we have–cable modem service from x. We have these business areas, and here's our plan for a business park we plan to develop. Here are the kinds of businesses we're looking to attract. Here's what our education and medium income levels are. What should our cities be looking at? We're trying to get information from vendors that we can look at it and see what makes sense. Do we have the fastest speeds we need or is there any way to increase that? Are prices such that, if we encourage another competitor, we'll be able to get better service and better choices?"

Vendors can give you the technology briefings you need to understand the basics of the various technologies and their capabilities. But the government owes it to taxpayers to do the much of their homework upfront and figure out what it is that they want. Take your time and use internal resources to be thorough as you collect the information Before you issue an RFI, ask one or two vendors what type of information is important in order for them to draft a response that fits a community's specific needs.

To Sum It Up

Now that we've looked at the emphasis that needs to be placed on learning from your constituents what their needs are, it should be clear this is an element of the implementation process where you don't want to skimp on effort or resources. However, don't get so tied up gathering feedback that you never move the project forward.

Follow a structured needs analysis framework that can be replicated by all of your stakeholders to organize everyone's thinking, areas of focus and ideas that are produced. Use categories of tactics to further organize ideas that are generated, and the actions that people plan to take as you pursue broadband deployment. Adapt as necessary to everyone's unique needs. With everyone following the same process, this will help the various parties stay on track and collectively finish this phase.

As you work through this process, consider the suggestion from Paul Butcher, Intel's Marketing Manager, State and Local Governments, that you "create some type of auditable assumptions, and use financial records to support those assumptions. Make sure you standardize benchmarks and values. Then have an accounting firm come in and verify to the taxpayers the validity of your numbers. This would be an exciting way to let constituents know that you've done your homework well, and there is sound fiscal basis for advancing your pursuit of broadband."

CHAPTER 7

Aligning Technology with Business Needs

The great challenge of large-scale technology projects is aligning the most appropriate technology with business needs. And by business needs, I mean what it is that all of the stakeholders and users of the network (including government) want to accomplish. Sometimes project teams get so fixated with the technical requirements, or the capabilities of the latest, hottest technologies that they forget about the people who actually have too use the finished solution.

I'm a big advocate of going into the needs assessment process with few preconceived notions of what the best broadband technology is for a community. During the broadband stimulus process you'd see this blog or that column stating unequivocally that fiber is the only true broadband solution. Or for rural communities, wireless is the only thing that makes financial sense. This jumping the gun can get you into big trouble. For example, what made WiFi in 2006 the Britney Speers of municipal broadband technologies was the hype that presented WiFi as the cure for every social ill under the sun: unemployment, low tourist numbers, young people abandoning communities, etc.

Like Britney before two marriages, two children and too much marketing, WiFi was a star, but with a specific value for a specific audience that shouldn't have been promoted outside of that niche. Once the reality of the technology's limitations relative to people's inflated expectations set in, couple with private companies' really bad business models, there were a dozen or two major network project flameouts and a ton of bad press. This chapter presents some guidelines to help you avoid a similar flameout.

Ten Business-Side Tips for Getting the Best From It

Regardless of how the project team for a broadband project is structured, there should be one or more individuals who have IT expertise and a designated role to manage the technology aspects of the project. From my interviews over past years, it's often the city or county CIO who's in this position. Someone who's previously had a few years of tech experience usually has a decent handle on aligning technology with business needs. However, for the business side of a project team, this could be their first technology adventure. Here's some advice for them to maximize the value that IT people and tech consulting firms offer.

Effective alignment begins with your state of mind

1. IT is neither your enemy nor your beast of burden. As long as everyone realizes they're all working ultimately for the community's success (and acts like it), then you get effective end results. IT people have legitimate responsibility for the operation and security of the technology systems that are put in place with the network so it operates effectively, efficiently and profitably. They also likely know more about what works and doesn't work from a technical perspective. Find common ground to make the technology and IT resources work for you, not common cause to gripe, moan and complain.

Conversely, the business side must be willing to build bridges, as well as treat the IT people across the table as equal partners. These aren't people who sling code and lay cable at your beck and call. IT folks are very creative at using technology and solving problems. Respect them for their talent and treat them the same as any director or manager sitting across from you. And whatever you do, be reasonable with your deadlines. Neither Rome nor any broadband application worth paying for was built in a day.

2. You don't need to know programming, but you must understand some IT processes. Spend time informally with an IT person learning about their basic issues regarding broadband technology, programming, vendor options, etc. You'll better comprehend how an implementation will achieve your business objectives. Despite the marketing hype, different broadband technologies have limitations, which is typical of all technologies. If you have a good grasp of their limitations, you'll do a better job of uncovering the potential benefits specific to your constituents because you won't expect the technology to do more than it can. Also, knowing how IT people do that voodoo that they do so well helps you better direct and evaluate their efforts.

Lean towards simplicity and prioritization

3. Reduce business needs to terms your mother will understand. Be simple and direct about what you want the technology to do. Few people have trouble understanding the goal if you tell them "we need a broadband app that lets our inspectors complete and submit citation paperwork, as well as print violations at building sites." You don't have to solve every business problem in one implementation. In fact, it's much better if you try to solve one or two, bask in the ROI glory of that success and quickly move on to the next problem–as long as you have a well defined roadmap for the entire technology implementation process.

4. Demand functionality a sixth grader can use. Regardless of the application's complexity, the user interface must be simple whether we're talking about an application to manage the network, or an application to be accessed over the network. Be dogmatic about this. Nothing kills ROI faster than people refusing to use an application that's difficult to access or operate. You don't control what people see and do on the Internet, but subscribers have to get there from your network. Network access commands, screen prompts and data requests should use terminology the average constituent can understand.

5. Don't ask for it all, all at once. Few things cause delays, cost overruns and disappointments like the "everything-but-the-kitchen-sync" approach to network and application design. Except maybe its ugly stepchild, Feature Creep–that continual adding of "gee-wouldn't-this-be-nice" features. Lay down the law, particularly to the top brass–no requests to IT for new features once the project starts! That's why there's version 2.0, even with a broadband network.

Be clear on your business objectives

6. The application needs to help stakeholders increase revenues, save money or run a better organization. If you can't align project objectives within at least one of these categories, why waste IT's time? Conversely, whenever IT recommends a broadband-related project, be sure they justify it using these criteria. Not only will IT develop a better solution, you also make it easier for everyone to measure success. Going back to item #3. Printing a violation on-site is a clear definition of what you want an application to do. But if printing the violation isn't going to save time because you still have to send it via snail mail to some location, the feature may not be worth its extra cost.

7. Accelerate or eliminate processes. You're not, hopefully, creating solutions to execute isolated tasks. You're building, even if it's in stages or is comprised of several technologies, one broadband infrastructure to smooth out wrinkles in your stakeholders' business operating procedures, or enable individuals to achieve a myriad of personal goals.

While it's true that building a network that moves data in megabits or gigabits per second is one key measures of a project's success, you are also transforming how organizations and people in your community go about their business. Be clear with IT about which overarching business and personal processes are being addressed. When the IT group can see the big picture, they'll develop the most appropriate network and broadband applications to meet the needs of your constituents.

8. Improve lines of communication to various end-user audiences. Implementing a successful broadband network depends on getting a significant percentage of your primary stakeholders and target market to use it. When you meet with the IT group to plan your implementation, clearly define a process for IT to gather feedback from end users about how they do their jobs, what their operational and personal needs are and as the application is tested and deployed, what works and what doesn't.

Also create a mechanism for regular on-going communication among stakeholders and general subscribers, as well as from those on the business side of the project team. However, open and frequent communication does not open the door for the business side to micromanage IT. If one of your finance team stands up during a meeting and starts doing network design on the whiteboard, you might want to keep on eye on that crew. Next thing you know, they'll be out in the streets directing crews in bucket trucks.

Be clear on quantifying and qualifying results...

9. Ideally, every objective has measurable benchmarks. While it's best to be able to quantify the dollar impact of your deployment, sometimes it's enough to quantify the changes, such as number of government worker tasks reduced, hospital ER visits reduced through telemedicine, home based businesses created, etc. The key is to have stakeholders, constituents and IT agree on what network results you're measuring and what are the metrics for success.

10. Even "warm & fuzzy" has a measure for success. Broadband may not be about the money, but rather constituent or employee satisfaction with service improvement. That's fine as long as everyone's agreed on what the objectives are and how they will be measured. The business side should feel comfortable setting up some sort of metrics to gage these intangible successes. How many constituents sent you letters of support? Can we double referrals of businesses looking to relocate/expand their physical plan operations? Have we won awards for achievements such as best community for jobs?

It Takes Two to Tango—IT's Role in the Relationship

Of course, IT also has a role in making sure their relationship with the business side goes smoothly. There are more elements of a broadband implementation than with typical technology applications, including politics, state and federal regulators, competitors using the same infrastructure and unfavorable geography. IT therefore has to work closely with managers to make sure all these moving parts are well coordinated so they come together for maximum effect. IT also has to aggressively manage expectations about what the technology can and can't do so there isn't much wailing and gnashing of teeth during and after the project.

If you look to some of the commercial entities that have deployed sizeable wireless applications, there are valuable lessons to learn. Joyce Lewis, the Sr. IT Director for an international banking company, followed a rather defined process for keeping executives in sync with a major wireless project. You may be able to adapt this to your project.

She used a requirements investigation process in which her team initially sat down with the business "customer" and stepped through in detail what they believed they wanted. In this stage IT just listened and gathered information, then went away to analyze technology options that would meet the needs identified. Next they did a market comparison of solutions from different vendors and evaluated different versions of one vendor's product.

"Based on these activities we created high-level project plans so our team could speak in an organized way to the main business stakeholder and the person who controlled the purse strings for that department about what the project might entail. On the tech side we would have a detail-level technician and project manager. If the business customer decided they wanted to move on the project, it would get funding. Some business unit managers had sign off authority, while other projects needed to go up to Finance and Purchasing. We would also determine if people on either the business or the IT side could implement the project alone or needed outside consultants."

If you're going to operate in similar fashion, be sure to include a clear picture of the good, the bad and the potentially ugly aspects of the initiative. Gregory Morrison, VP & CIO of media heavyweight Cox Enterprises, Inc. has his IT team educate executives on the possibilities and liabilities of the technology. He finds that when senior managers develop an intuitive understanding of what technology can and cannot do, their requests tend to be more realistic. To this end, Mr. Cox's team creates a steering committee of business unit leaders and IT management.

Getting inside of each other's head

Broadband deployments on a city- or countywide scale can take up to a year or more to complete when starting from scratch. Have IT put processes in place so they know what the business side sees as things change. Depending on how aggressive broadband business plans are, or how quickly needs might change as the network comes online, determined how frequently IT and department units should meet.

Keep IT informed about what changes, including political ones, are affecting the stakeholders' operations that the network will impact. The business side needs to know about new tech developments such as upgrades, delays in vendors' product plans and new applications that can improve the network's ability to generate revenue.

Understand the personal motivations and agendas of all of the people involved. Sometimes politicians and other stakeholders foolishly want to be too aggressive using a particular technology for no other reason than to have bragging rights. We saw a lot of this in the municipal wireless days when politicians had to be "the first" with such and such, or promise the biggest network northeast of the Pecos, showing little common sense in their decision-making. Or they'll reject the most tried and true technology option because there's some new fad that's getting airtime. This is where folks can really get themselves into trouble. IT often hopes that wisdom and logic prevail, but sometimes they have to make a career-effecting decision on how hard they want to press an issue.

Business people need to understand that technological purists drive some IT interests, and respond accordingly. For example, consider the time when people began implementing UNIX years ago. It was a superb communication platform. It did exactly what it was supposed to. But it was not user friendly, and it wasn't easy to find skilled people who could implement and support UNIX. While the tech person wants it because it's good technology, a business manager needs to intervene sometime to show how and why it's not good for their people who have to use it.

To be or not to be. That is the alignment question

We can also learn some important lessons from municipal government managers. Philadelphia's former Acting License and Inspection Commissioner Robert Solvibile worked on that department's mobile workforce application deployment. Their IT team implemented a pretty extensive effort to align technology with needs. Each unit of L & I identified 24 processes they wanted to automate with the software. "First we created the 'As Is' document to see what we were doing," states Solvibile. "We brought in all of the clerical staff and anybody else involved in the process to tell us how things worked."

In those same meetings the manager and the clerical people created the "To Be" document. This detailed everything the units wanted including all of the bells and whistles. Next the Deputy Commissioners and supervisors were added to this group to get their agreement that this was what they wanted as well. Then the Commissioner and his Deputy would sign off on the final list and the vendor's staff began preliminary work on the software.

Solvibile observes that, "like anything else, once people see what they want implemented start to take shape, they begin asking 'what if we did this?' We'd make suggestions for improvements based on feedback while our staff went through a system of testing the 'To Be' features. They ran various examples of work projects and entered certain problems into the software to see how it reacted. And then we would change things and try a different problem."

During this process, but before moving to final programming, the department's staff and the programming staff each created a written document of understanding as to what the respective groups expected the final outcome to be. Finally there was a "clarity conference" to make sure everyone was speaking the same language.

These procedures may seem to be excessively compulsive, but most business executives and IT managers who've been through a less than financially rewarding deployment will tell you they wished they had been as thorough. Nothing's guaranteed except death and taxes, but you can be reasonably assured that this degree of attention to aligning broadband technologies and applications to your workers' needs saves you lots of money and grief while leading to a more productive work force in the long term.

Aligning Technology Initiatives with Community Needs

One thing that will determine a city's or county's credibility early in the deployment process is the quality of the network's service as it comes online. As you make decisions, Butcher encourages you to keep in mind the reasons you decided to build the network.

"There are probably thousands of ways you can use the technology, so don't try to do everything. What are the top choices for your constituents? Once you have this, go through your inventory of technology assets and determine what's there to help you support constituents' needs. Do some spectral analysis and find out if there's any noise out there that can interfere with wireless technology you or constituents are thinking about using. Pull all this information together and make final decisions about which technologies makes the most sense."

Also important is the quality of service and support (a.k.a. political cover) you give to community leaders and others who become your champions facilitating deployment. This can present significant management challenge if you're proposing a range of applications and programs to need from diverse constituent groups. However, keep in mind that by publicly embracing broadband and your team's plan, these leaders are putting some of their reputation and maybe even money on the line for a project that may take many months before the benefits are fully realized.

While you are lining up community champions, be sure they are aware of the technology's limitations. For example, WiFi signals only travel but so far. They will penetrate some surfaces but not other and heavy foliage affects signals, so business offices or residences may need bridging devices. WiMAX signals cover greater distances, but can be more costly both for the network operator and subscribers. I strongly advise you to prepare written materials for community leaders that outline the basic technology requirements for end users to participate on the network. Remember the rules for communicating needs to non-tech people: use terms your mother can understand.

Patricia DeCarlo says "Don't tell me I need a CPE. Write it down. What's it called, how big does it have to be, who sells it, how much does it costs? I have a very high opinion of myself and I assume that my stupid questions are a whole bunch of other people's stupid questions. When I go to Radio Shack, or Staples, I would not have a clue what to say to those people, what to ask for. I need someone to do a one-page flyer that tells people if you have a computer and you want to access broadband, this is what you need to buy to make it work."

Taking it to the streets

To determine what technologies can best address constituents' needs, Archer Perry believes "you ask them the question 'what is it that you want to get done?' and then work together with them to find the right answer. I talked to everyone I met in the community about the value of broadband, and once people understood what it was, they thought of ideas and talked to their friends who came up with more ideas. Finding a win/win opportunity for virtually anyone is fairly easy to figure out."

When I do research and interview people who are new to a particular technology I want to educate them about, I typically start with the question, how are you doing such and such now? As they respond I might probe a little to understand why they do something a particular way, or what would their ideal process be to do that task. As they respond, you can usually find points where the technology can deliver or facilitate that particular process, or something close to it.

An example of creating winning opportunities comes from DeCarlo as she explained a serious communication challenge her group has. "Getting information out in this neighborhood is a very time consuming and expensive proposition because the newspapers don't cover what's going on in the neighborhood, not even the local Latino newspaper. So whenever we need to be in touch with the neighborhood, which is over 10,000 people, you have to create and distribute flyers. To be sure the message gets delivered you go out, knock on doors and explain things to people. You have to go to the corner stores and bodegas to talk to people so they'll talk to the neighbors who come into the stores later. All of that and you still don't know how many people know about the event."

Patricia and others in her neighborhood didn't understand at first what an Internet community portal is. But after the representative from the City explained it was a technology tool that is specific to the neighborhood that gets the word out faster and easier than the process Patricia described, its value hit home. For them, because portals are neighborhood based, the technology made a lot of sense. She then was able to work with the vendor to figure out different applications that the neighborhood can use.

Community organizations you work with need to step back to see not only what the neighborhood wants, but also how the organization itself can use broadband to facilitate the services that they provide ton constituents. How can their organization grow and become more efficient using broadband? There's a lot of thinking and a lot of asking required. How are they going to pay for all of this technology? How are these portals maintained?

As she learned more about the possibilities of broadband, Patricia started generating ideas to help the association. "We have the child care center and after-school program, but people need to come over with paperwork to enroll their kids and hope that the person they need to see is there. I'm wondering, would it make sense for parents to enroll their children in these programs or make appointments with housing counselors over the Internet, and not have to go to the office to complete paperwork? This is something that would work for us and for folks in the neighborhood."

The big juggling act

One obvious challenge to a network's success is that you need these community and business organizations to carry much of the load getting constituents to use broadband once it's in place. However, some of them may not have the technical skills on staff or money in respective budgets to make it happen, and your project team likely won't have enough staff to get it done. Shortly after deciding to pursue broadband, give thought to these challenges. It's likely part of the solution lies in pulling together the right team of vendors and service providers who can work with your point people in the communities to help align the right technologies and also teach constituents how to use it.

As your people work with the various constituencies, be sure they encourage groups to prioritize the many ideas that are sure to come up, giving preference to those that can be implemented easily and with easy-to-achieve benefits. The larger the municipality or county, the more diverse is the range of products and services running over the network. You need simple initiatives to minimize the strain on your resources, particularly while the infrastructure while it is being built out, tested and refined.

A member of the Executive Committee, Ed Schwartz, believes these small community initiatives spawns subsidiary projects that in and of themselves are beneficial. "These types of projects open the doors to other creative ways to use the technology, and frankly, other sources of funding. You could see support from national corporations that otherwise wouldn't have bothered with a particular community. I also think a broadband project that is cast as an economic development initiative can be a lure for federal and state contracts."

Exploring Technology Alignment Options

Every community will have to uncover what type of applications and content makes sense to benefit their various constituents, and subsequently what type of technology will need to be in place. This section addresses four areas of community interest that likely will drive projects and gives you come food for thought. This isn't a complete list, but some good starting points.

Improving health and public safety

At both the city and county levels, consider seriously how broadband integrates the city public safety organizations such as police and fire departments with their county counterpart agencies, as well as hospitals and other medical facilities. As we saw with 9/11 and four years later on the Gulf Coast, how well these entities coordinate communication amongst themselves impacts the quality of service that health care providers deliver. Or what the lack of that alignment means.

On their own, many health care facilities are deploying broadband in one form or another to improve how they deliver and manage patient care. Some digital divide initiatives currently underway are designed to improve citizens' access to important health care information, and improve medical professionals' ability to communicate with citizens.

The next step is to leverage the broadband network so health care providers can be a better resource to public safety personnel in the field, especially during large-scale emergencies. Ambulance services such as American Medical Response and fire and rescue personnel such as those in San Diego are integrating their patient and business management applications into various wireless technologies to improve patient care at the scene and en route to the hospital. These applications should mesh nicely with broadband efforts in most communities.

Part of the alignment process depends a lot on asking the right questions. How can the technology increase first responders' access to knowledge on the Internet and elsewhere that helps them provide better medical assistance in the field? Can emergency personnel use the network to tap into city or county information, such as layouts of large building complexes or details on hazardous materials, which can be relayed to hospital personnel to bring their expertise to bear? What will local government need to do to make its data easier to access while ensuring data security?

Evaluate the various options to push emergency-related information through the network to the mobile devices of residents, care givers and public safety personnel. In addition to the federal government's efforts, cities and counties need to factor this type of application into their plans.

One application that doesn't get enough attention in the discussion of broadband is embedded wireless devices that can go into assets such as infusion pumps, monitors, fire fighting equipment and the multitude of assets needed to deal with disasters. If you can use the network to improve healthcare and emergency response organizations' ability to track the location and movement of these assets, you immediately strengthen the security umbrella over your community. This also can put your community in line to secure government funds to offset costs of network deployment.

Economic advancement for the business community

To fully align technology initiatives with economic development needs requires long-term planning and patience because economic improvement can take months or even a couple of years to become notable in ways you can measure. What's more, a lot of the success you experience in this area depends on the actions of parties that are responsible for policy programs and technology applications that impact local economies, but may not be subscribers to the network.

David Keyes, Community Technology Program Manager for the City of Seattle, WA's IT Department points out two such applications. "One category of applications is comprised of those that reduce the time spent waiting for data transmissions and the delivery of services. We were able to provide a Cambodian women's association with cable broadband service, which made a huge difference in them being able to retrieve online the case records they need to file for state benefits on behalf of their clients. Subsequently they can see more clients in a day.

"Another category is comprised of applications that increase local companies' ability to reach markets globally. In a state-funded project in Ferry County, a group called Stone Soup has been putting people from rural areas and their products online, and helping them set up e-commerce pages. You can see them at www.shopthefrontier.com.

"A third category of applications consists of those that enable companies to perform interactive tasks such as video conferencing with customers. I can bring someone into Seattle via the Web who has a special skill but happens to live in Philly. This increases the capacity for learning for local business owners who have a harder time leaving their companies for seminars and the like."

The key to getting the broadband infrastructure to open up new opportunities is motivating businesses to spend time learning how to use the technology. Home-based businesses, mom and pop retailers and small sole proprietor operations may already have computers. The content these constituents need is information to help them improve how they work and tools to leverage the Net as a gateway to the world. Community-oriented portals should be helpful in driving foot and online traffic to these merchants. However, content and links made possible, though not necessarily created, by the city's efforts is the catalyst for business improvement by companies of all sizes.

When you have several equal needs within a community competing for resources, constituents get caught up in no-win situations. The challenge to project teams wanting to create win-win situations, then, is to be a conduit for broadband and content resources that help businesses grow, but also make sure that these resources are equitably available, reliable and add value. The local chambers of commerce, tourism boards and local chapters of business associations are the likely partners to help you determine what technologies can help them.

Also give businesses the means to create their own solutions. De-Carlo adds, "if our people can come up with other ideas, this would be wonderful. I would like to have a page with two columns. In the 'A' column is a list from the experts saying you can do this, this and this. Then we show this column to the neighborhood and in the 'B' column they say, out of that list we'd like to do these projects and develop that service, or whatever."

Bridging the digital divide

Alignment in support of facilitating digital inclusion is complicated by the fact that any effective solution in this area requires a combination of resources besides technology. From 2004–2006, discussions about closing the divide focused on giving people access to the Net and often ended there, as if handing people Internet access accounts would miraculously raise their economic status. This isn't a problem you address with a drop-it-off-and-leave solution.

To the benefit of everyone involved, the broadband stimulus program as well as the FCC's effort to write a national broadband strategy threw light on the real path to digital inclusion. Technology is only the first element of the equation you have to put into place. Digital Impact Group (formerly Wireless Philadelphia) CEO Greg Goldman has found through several years of experience that "a meaningful program must address all four main barriers to underserved communities participating in the digital economy: complexity, cost, literacy [technical competency with hardware and software] and the lack of experience using the Internet. The packaging of hardware, training and tech support with Internet access is what's needed to accomplish this so low-income individuals can cross the divide."

It's fairly safe to say that only with stakeholders working together with the network project team will you determine the complete range of technologies and related resources that get matched with constituents. Project teams can then build broadband infrastructure across neighborhoods of all economic strata as long as they've secured the funds for building the network, and have a business case for sustaining it. There may be a few rural communities where low-income areas would get wireless because it's cheaper to build while other neighborhoods get wired services, but I expect there'd be some political backlash to this.

Partners from the business and nonprofit communities may be the ones who underwrite the cost of building broadband infrastructure in low-income communities of cities that do not plan to build a citywide network. Corporate partnerships plus sponsorships from large technology vendors may be the path to getting software and new or refurbished hardware into constituents' hands. Nonprofits and community service organizations are often the partners implementing training programs or providing services that help clients maximize their newfound skills to open educational and personal economic development opportunities.

During the process you have to ask these and other questions if you want to make digital inclusion a reality. Who are you going to partner with to bring in or facilitate delivery of the needed resources, and do they have a track record of success? Do these potential partners have proven technology skills to provide what's needed, as well as the ability to foresee some of the advances in the various technologies needed. You don't want to spend money to bring people into the digital economy but then push them into dead end careers

As partners define their plans, and you establish with them their respective responsibilities, be sure your IT people are aware of the partners' technology issues in case some part of the network infrastructure needs to be adjusted to address them. Define the role that social services, economic development or other departments and their Web sites will play in the communities' overall plans.

An important side note here. I believe there should be some charge to citizens for the services that evolve from broadband initiatives, even if the charge for hardware and access is just a few dollars a month. The goal here is to close the digital divide so individuals can take more control of improving their economic condition and advancing their lives. You only foster dependency of a different sort if you give people everything for free.

To Sum It Up

There are so many elements to matching the right applications to the various needs that it may be difficult to decide which direction to move first. The key is to always return to the main objectives of the initiative, prioritize based on where you can get some early wins and build momentum and keep the feedback flowing.

After exploring ways to align technology with needs, the test of whether you made the right decision comes through a series of pilot projects. The next chapter gives some details on how you can maximize their use.

CHAPTER 8

Take Me to the Pilot Project

The pilot project is the process of taking a subset of the total geo-graphical area an organization plans to cover with broadband and building out the technology (or technologies) the project team has in mind for full deployment. Pilots test the ability of the products to perform as promised and withstand the rigors of the environment in which they will operate. They also can be an opportunity to test some of the applications that will run over the network, in part to test the validity of the assumptions about the potential ROI that deploying the network will generate.

For technology in general, the technical capability and ROI assumptions often are tested at the same time, while other organizations only test one of these because they are pretty certain of either the capabilities or the ROI. With broadband networks, you'll probably use pilots mainly to test capability. The value of a pilot project to validate ROI projections depends on what qualifies as success. If improving economic development is a metric, for example, it's difficult for a pilot to make enough of an impact in areas such as transforming the workforce for a digital economy unless you ran the pilot for several years. It's do-able, but not particularly practical.

You can run a collection of pilots for specific stakeholder and general constituent applications or broadband adoption programs, but the format for these and the criteria by which they are judged is likely to be all over the map. Your universities or school districts may have clear metrics for showing student and school workforce improvements from wireless broadband. The other stakeholders, the business case is not always cut and dry. The benefits of government and community efforts to improve quality of life issues is not easily quantifiable, yet somehow you have to reconcile the fact that taxpayers demand some level of accountability.

Pilot Projects 101

In a general sense, pilot projects are merely a dress rehearsal for the rollout of a major technology implementation. A lot of the process involves technology testing by the IT members of your project team who get eyeballs-deep into the bits and bytes of a software program or the chipsets and switches of the hardware. They're trying to make sure each component works well on its own and integrated with other applications.

As an administrator or director on the business side, the primary questions you want the pilot to answer are 1) can people use the technology effectively, 2) what will it cost to get it deployed and have people use it effectively and 3) will the benefits you expect likely be the benefits you get? These questions apply for the community network, stakeholder applications and community or constituent service programs such as moving low-income individuals onto the Internet to receive skills training. The mechanics and logistics for determining the answers vary widely for pilots in each category.

Pilot for the broadband network

Here's a good point to present, in general layperson's terms, the main components of a broadband network infrastructure that makes up the "last mile" that I described in Chapter 2. There are three: the edge, a middle tier and the distribution tier.

The edge of a wireless network is where the radio transmitters are placed around the city or county, typically on light and telephone poles. There may be thousands of them in a large city communicating to mobile devices equipped with plug-in cards or embedded communication chips, sensors placed in physical assets such as cameras or utility meters.

In the middle tier is a collection of gateways where all of the data gets delivered to and picked up from the access points. These may hang on telephone poles and the like, but sometimes these sit on rooftops and water towers that place them in good positions to receive transmitters' signals. The combined collection of edge and middle tier technologies is often referred to as the mesh.

The distribution tier is the communication bridge between all of the gateways and the point of presence (POP) that in turn transmits the city's data to and from the Internet. For this tier of the network, one option is to create a sonic ring of redundant microwave links between six or seven communication towers. Each tower has a massive highspeed link to the POP, and data flows back and forth between the towers and the gateways.

Test these infrastructure components of the network through what can be referred to as a "proof of concept" (POC) in which a square mile or less is built out with all of the component parts. Then people are informed that they can stop by with their mobile devices and see how the network operates. Though the line between a POC and a pilot seems to be a bit blurry, the former is primarily about showing that the technology can indeed work and pilots push the networks to show to what extent the technology will work. The difference is similar to doing a test drive around the block a few times versus driving a car across the state over different terrains while testing all of the features and alternating between hauling passengers, cargo and a trailer.

Besides making everyone comfortable with the vendors involved, a POC is a good way for the business side to get stakeholders and constituents to understand what you plan to put in place and recruit supporters by giving them a sense of the benefits. The buildout process gives you some initial insight to the time and logistics that will be involved rolling the infrastructure out to the entire city or county. However, don't feel obligated to do a POC, particularly if you're in a hurry. You may find it better to just jump fully into a pilot.

After the POC…

For the IT side, the pilots primarily consist of running extensive performance tests to understand topography issues, how the network handles huge numbers of users, the impact of climate changes and other technical features. These test results give the business side a better idea of final network deployment costs and operational issues such as equipment requirements or coverage limitations that stakeholders and communities must address with vendors.

"Establish up front clear criteria on what you intend to study and what you want to get out of the pilot," says Cole Reinwand, Program Lead at one of the major telecom companies. "An approach such as 'come over, put the network up and we'll see how it performs' won't cut it. You must be specific about what your needs are. What are you ultimately trying to do? Set a fairly strict timeline for the pilot to establish these criteria."

John Dolmetsch of Business Information Group cautions that, "you need to have a well thought out plan regarding the city assets where you expect vendors to mount the equipment. In different cities, access to the light poles has been a problem. This wasn't a forethought but rather an afterthought because cities thought they owned the rights to these, and they even told us that they did. We've started pilots and then found out that one of the local utilities in fact owns them, so the cities had to go through various procedures to gain access. Make sure before you bring in a vendor that you can use different mountings whether on buildings or poles. If you can't, approach the owners first and negotiate all those issues."

To that end, a city or county needs at least one staff member to be on the project team as a dedicated point person who interacts with the vendors and be a go between for various local government agencies. In the pilot stage some in the agencies may not understand what you're trying to do, so it's very difficult to expect the vendors to go to each department and ask for access to the poles, terminals and other resources. Along with a single point of contact, have an open process for gathering feedback from vendors throughout the pilot.

Constituent pilot projects

Some primary goals of constituent pilots (testing applications and programs that rely on the network) are to show how they successfully use the network, determine how well the infrastructure supports these projects and create a blueprint for other groups to follow. The project team probably won't be as involved with constituent projects once the network is fully deployed, but in the early stages you want to ensure that you create a momentum for the community changes you're trying to affect.

There may be as many ways to run pilot projects as there are constituent groups. This creates challenges in the beginning, but as you run focus groups and town meetings, the types of projects that constituents really want to develop bubble up to the top of priority lists.

To establish criteria to test for in these pilots, refer to your main goals for the broadband network. If the main objective is economic development, then set up pilot projects that draw community businesses onto the network or drive customers to businesses using the network. If an objective is to increase parents' involvement with their children's computer-driven coursework, then develop pilots that reach out to parents living near a particular school and give them free Internet access during the pilots.

It is vitally important to track pilot results. How many neighborhood residents logged onto the Internet for the first time? What was the impact in terms of people using the network to find jobs, get responses from City Hall or other quantifiable activities? How many stores used the commerce-generating portal and what was the impact on retail sales? Quantify the number of students receiving technology training who are answering tech support questions from residents.

These pilots are where you can push your creativity to the limit, though you do want to limit the number of pilot projects while the wrinkles get worked out. Besides providing the early successes that increase community support for full deployment, also use the pilots to fine-tune the list of technology issues that need to be addressed in other constituency groups and ferret out potential roadblocks to broadband adoption.

"However, I would offer a word of caution," says Scott Shamp, Director of the Grady College New Media Institute at the University of Georgia and driving force behind Athens, GA's original downtown WiFi deployment. "Some end users unfortunately develop expectations that can be divergent from the intended purpose of the wireless initiative. If a constituent tells you that your system doesn't do 'X' when you really designed the system to do 'Y', then it is important that you put your feedback into the proper context for them. Don't let criticism distract you from what you want to accomplish with your project." At the same time, always be mindful of that you have to constantly manage expectations, even when people support your initiatives.

Communities have to look at a core of reputable technology providers during their pilot. They shouldn't limit their review to a single vendor or necessarily to a single technology type. WiFi might not be the right solution a rural community looking at video surveillance even though it is highly touted for big-city networks, for example. Communities should describe the desired applications and resulting benefits, but leave it to vendors to propose and justify what technology best serves that need.

Don't ignore existing infrastructure when setting up your pilots. I read one consultant's financial assessment in which he recommended replacing existing highspeed lines with another technology because it would be cheaper than paying those recurring service charges. Cheaper, yes. But is it prudent? Morrow County, OR kept their dual-fiber-lines infrastructure in place and integrated WiFi in their deployment so they have super-high speed backhaul for the wireless applications and redundancy. As much as you can, take advantage of current complementary technology before actually replacing it.

Life's little challenges…

"On the community side where we did portals, we learned that it takes lots of feet on the street meeting with groups, explaining what the program is, showing them how this can help them meet their goals," Dianah Neff states. "It was more than we thought would be necessary. How do you get these community players who don't usually collaborate working together? You need to have multiple pilots going on so you can move forward in some areas while waiting for others. Some neighborhoods just take longer to follow through on their plans."

Processing payments from low-income individuals for Internet access is a potential issue since quite a few don't have credit cards to use once they are online, or even checking accounts. Depending on who actually runs your network, the logistics of facilitating and managing alternative sources of payments could catch you by surprise since network access is usually free during the initial pilots. Prepaid service cards are an option to resolve this payment challenge, but an infrastructure needs to be put in place to manage this option, which itself needs to be pilot tested.

Smaller towns not part of a multi-community project that want to pilot test a range of product options have to consider that they might be ignored by larger vendors with broader product lines because small installations aren't financially rewarding. However Shamp implies that it's better to hold out and wait for the right vendor than to rush through with product purchase without some sort of product testing.

"The biggest lesson I learned from our pilot is the value of working with a vendor who understands and can accommodate your specific implementation challenges. Don't work with a vendor if you find out they're trying to wing it by using what it already makes and those products don't meet your needs." If you have to wait for vendors to pay attention to you, look for alternatives or be patient. Don't settle for inadequate products, and be leery of vendors who aren't used to working with your type of community.

There can be dozens of potential constituent pilot projects for large multi-city or multi-county projects with ambitious social agendas for the technology. When you can, use the early pilots to create a foundation that communities can build on to deliver services over that network. However, you can't use a cookie cutter approach in every neighborhood. You have different cultures, languages levels of poverty or literacy, etc. There's a balancing act here between not re-inventing the wheel and dealing with the uniqueness of your constituents.

Survey your communities to see how much expertise is within their groups to run a pilot. Ninth Wave Media's President Judy Miller says, "There are often one or two people who have some level of technology expertise, or might be willing to learn the basics of using Web-based software or motivating/training people to go online. Assign a technology liaison from the project team to work with whoever is running the community pilot activities. Then it's a matter of determining how in-depth the community pilot leaders wants to go, how much do they want to learn and so forth.

Consider asking the vendors to step up and provide some hands-on support to help communities test Internet portals and other software applications that you plan to run on the network. Another potential support group are your public service agencies that may be involved with programs such as welfare-to-work assistance. In an area that is running a pilot for network infrastructure, see if different agencies or nonprofit organizations will provide online access to their services for their clients in this area for the duration of the pilot.

Can You Really Get There from Here?

Give or take a few days, one woman delivers a baby in nine months. But you can't get nine women together to deliver a baby in one month. However, when it comes to technology, some managers estimate the ROI of the final deployment with the "nine women/one-month" philosophy. "If 50 employees use the application to generate $10,000 in time savings during the pilot, it's a given we'll generate $100,000 when we deploy to 500 workers." If you carry this type of thinking to the broadband network project, will your pilot accurately predict the return on investment?

Well, maybe it will. Probably it won't. There are so many variables that affect a network, and so many ways in which subscribers can benefit, you are bound to over- or under-predict a few numbers. This is not to say that you won't generate enough benefits to justify the investment. But if local politicians or stakeholders spend a year or more expecting $1 million in ROI and you deliver $400,000, there could be some long faces around the table at performance review time.

This is an important point because the time between the pilot and the full rollout is your last best chance to make changes in projections about how much you're going to gain with this application and at what price. Once the deployment train leaves the station, it is much more expensive to respond to any major miscalculations in pilot-generated assumptions.

How much time should you spend on doing an extensive analysis to project financial ROI versus a simple extrapolation exercise? It depends. How closely will you be held accountable for the projected ROI numbers? Some communities are happy if they just see any marked improvement in the metrics that are used to determine success (e.g. number of home-based businesses increasing 20% instead of 40%), while others want to see specific numbers met after deployment. The latter case is where you'll have to spend lots of hours with calculators and spreadsheets.

Of greater interest may be whether or not you can complete the deployment within budget. What happens when each cost of deploying a 1-square mile pilot is extrapolated out to 10 square miles, 50 or several hundred square miles that cross four or five counties? What new logistics-related costs come into play? It may not be expensive to provide replacement parts for a network covering a quarter mile for a 90-day pilot. But infrastructure covering large geographical areas can drive the annual logistics costs for replacing and repairing parts or upgrading components way beyond an exponential increase in pilot costs. Have you and the vendor calculated properly?

Just as important as it is to accurately extrapolate infrastructure costs and their impact on ROI, you have to do the same thing for problems that pop up. The tendency for someone is to say "oh, one access point out of the 25 slipping out of its mount late in a pilot test, that's a minor problem. We can deal with it later." They don't want to delay the transition to deployment or they dread having to do another pilot. But as the commercial for a chain of auto repair shops says, "You can pay me now–or you can pay me later" after 10,000 access points are deployed and you have the same ratio of mount problems. (This is a strictly hypothetical equation, by the way.)

If you encounter what some might consider a small glitch, look at how much time it will cost for subscribers to work around the problem or burden your customer service people with calls and e-mails. One or two thousand people losing a couple of minutes each day becomes big bucks at the end of the year. Do more and better analysis during your pilot. Pay now or pay a lot more later.

To Sum It Up

The pilot project is probably a pivotal part of the any broadband deployment. This is the big test before you commit the big bucks to the technology you feel is going to make your initiatives a reality. In many cases, these pilots are your first and best opportunity to make a good impression, convert skeptics, recruit project champions and see how vendors' products work in the real world.

Take your time with both the planning and the execution of your pilots. Gather good feedback before, during and after your pilots. And if the pilot shows that some assumptions are a little off target, or a product or technology isn't quite fitting with how the stakeholders or community works, go back to the drawing board and do a new pilot. This can be the hardest thing for a project team to do because community broadband is very public and incredibly political right now.

"You have to look at how fast you jump into a technology that can potentially change how people work," advises Howard White, Deputy Building Official for St. John's County, Florida. "You shouldn't promise too much before it's been thoroughly tested. If you make expectations too high, then you can have a problem when reality sets in. Even with the newest application we're getting ready to release, which is really just a new feature we're adding, we have spent eight months making sure it will work before jumping out there."

From the beginning set the right expectations for everyone about how much time this process can take and remind people often throughout the pilot what it is you're trying to achieve. As the President of application service provider ServiceHub told me several years ago, "what you're buying with these pilot projects aren't your first steps of automation, but useful information to make better decisions. So run multiple pilots. Don't be afraid to pay your tuition for your education."

CHAPTER 9

Moving to Full Deployment

There comes a point when those driving broadband initiatives need to conclude that they've done sufficient planning and testing and it's time to move forward. Whether people realize when that point arrives is another story, given that they can always find something more that to add, review, guard against, etc.

As Digital Impact Group Board member Robert Bright sums it up, "without question, the more input you get when identifying constituents, customers, and so on, the better. You cannot ignore the political world given the lobbyists and incumbent businesses. You need to get a good understanding of what are the potential obstacles out there. But when I put my private industry hat on, I have to make decisions. I can't afford to circle on all of my decisions. Government will not move forward by continual circling."

When you ask, "does this address everyone's needs?" "Is it good for 'x' or 'y' organization?' "What if the incumbent wants to do this or that?" and get all of these questions answered, you end up spending a lot of time but you get useful information. However, do this too long and there's a point when you run out of gas. Bright remarks "we could still be doing the business plan today if we had looked at everything that's happened in the business world with broadband technology from one summer to the next."

This chapter is about moving forward. It captures a great deal of feedback from vendors and service providers involved with community network projects. These individuals also have years of experience overseeing deployment of large complex implementations leading-edge technologies. There's much to learn from them.

Engage All Engines—Make the RFP Process Work for You

Though your government may have developed RFPs for many technology deployments, few are similar to broadband implementations. Besides the wide range of computing devices and software you need to purchase, there are service providers, evolving network infrastructure issues, spectrum issues, business model options and community considerations you must address. This is not a job for the faint of heart and weak of planning skills.

When you start translating needs into an RFP, it's important to have the point person driving the RFP process do some filtering. A few cities may ask every local government departments and all of their stakeholders what they need, what would they do with a wireless network if it were in place, and so forth. Then they put every one of these requests into one RFP and say a vendor must be able to provide all of these services. Prioritize your list and restrict it to the top five-to-ten things that would be most helpful collectively by all stakeholders. If you ask for everything, the RFP could be just too expensive to respond to, or once the project starts everyone realizes it's impossible to complete without re-engineering the plan to water down elements of the system.

Doing thorough due diligence analysis on technology requests from stakeholder request, plus providing informative feedback helps keep your RFP reasonable. If a county supervisor thinks they need a gigabit-per-second connection, someone from your project team should say "you can't get that with most wireless technologies. You're thinking about capabilities better delivered by fiber." You want these kinds of issues addressed before they make it into the RFP. Otherwise vendors are in a bad spot, having to do a lot of time-consuming expensive stakeholder education, or perhaps committing to providing services that in reality they may not be able to deliver. It's hard for some vendors to say "no" to requirements in RFPs because they feel that saying "yes" to everything is going to help them to win the bid.

RFPs should reflect the broader vision

Rizwan Khaliq from IBM advises that your RFP reflects a broad strategic view. "Consider, for example, deployment of a public safety application. You may initially think of it being used for police and fire departments. But you look at a large county such as Miami Dade, the Gulf Coast region or some other areas that are exposed to natural disasters, a broadband network needs to get participation from multiple players beyond those under a municipality's umbrella. There are Federal or regional agencies that need to have access and be able to share data in real time with local officers. This is not a silo or vertical application."

What strategic view you have, and by default the view of the various stakeholders you consider in the needs analysis, is different based on where you are and what natural disasters you're likely to experience. Another factor that might affect this view could be terrorism, the potential for attacks on historical sites or vital infrastructure such as a nearby bridge that impacts the ability to move critical resources to where they're needed.

Your strategic view should include your business communities. Rizwan continues, "A government can look at how local companies could actually leverage the network for optimizing their business operations without compromising security. For example, in Rhode Island look at how CVS, which has a strong distribution center there, is leveraging their municipality's WiFi technology. A business in your area may want to optimize the network to maximize fleet management." This can be wrapped into the mission to make the city more economically attractive to local businesses.

Commercial and public service interests actually overlap in this example. Emergency first responders may point out the need to be able to communicate with a company in an emergency if they have petroleum or chemical supplies on their premises. Having the license data from all buildings plus floor plans and potentially hazardous inventories available to be sent to first responders can save time and lives. For a major area evacuation, these responders need to know what those business facilities look like before they get on the scene.

Is your point person in the know?

Given the mission critical nature of some of the city and county departments that access a wireless network in addition to other stakeholders, consider this advice from John Dolmetsch, President of system integrator Business Information Group. "Your RFP for wireless infrastructure should include similar requirements that have been in RFPs for deploying public safety wireless radio networks. There are established and documented procedures for the public sector that have been in place for 50 years now. Vendors need to respond to the RFP to build a WiFi or WiMAX network just as they would to these critical radio networks that have to be operational 24/7."

Another thing to consider is how much do the people driving the RFP process understand about the specifics of broadband technology and related issues. Are they willing to admit what they don't know? A lot of communities need to be realistic about this. If they have the skills internally to articulate the needs and write an RFP, that's great. But if they don't, then they need to recognize this and seek some third-party help. They can get in real trouble if they spec a system without really knowing what they're doing. They have one set of expectations of what the performance should be and the vendor has a different set. If the vendor feels they delivered to what they promised but the community's expectations haven't been met, then this obviously can create a serious problem.

As more deployments are launched, vendors are able to spot RFPs designed by individuals who don't have a good grip on the main issues, and one of two things may happen. When the size of the contract is enough or the vendor likes you, they may point out problem areas and help you re-work those. On the other hand, if the project team has under-scoped the budget to the point where they can't get what they want, vendors are smart enough to catch on and just won't bid on the project. What often happens with an organization in this latter category is that they go through the process, look at bids that do come in and maybe even run some trials. When these don't go well, the project team pulls the RFP and goes back to re-write the specs, scrap the program or find more budget.

Resist the temptation to use someone else's RFP to shortcut the process of defining your needs. Use them so you can figure out what you need to know and what you should be asking for from vendors. "Those who shorten the process end up confusing the private sector," observes Intel's Paul Butcher. "There was one major city that created an RFP that they did in a hurry and I heard about vendors walking away from it saying 'we can't respond to this.' If you want a good partner, you have to do your own homework."

Vendor Roundtable Offers Deployment Insights and Guidelines

To give you an overview of some of the key issues you should be considering, I brought some of the key vendors in the muni WiFi space into the discussion to share some insights. Included in the Q & A are:
Cole Reinwand, Program Lead, major telecom company, formerly with EarthLink

Paul Butcher, Intel–Marketing Manager–State and Local Governments, America's Marketing Group
Denise Barton, Tropos Networks –Director of Marketing
Craig Newman, Director of Business Development for Motorola's Canopy Wireless Broadband business
Rizwan Khaliq, Global Business Leader for IBM Digital Communities
John Dolmetsch, Business Information Group–President

It's important to have this input because these providers of technology and services are very much involved with the broadband initiatives of communities worldwide, including some international cities that are far along in their deployments. Their perspective is also valuable because they have a clearer view of the big picture issues, as well as the possible future direction of technology. There are some good tips here for selecting and working more effectively with vendors.

1. What do you feel is the role of a municipality and vendors/service providers in a partnership?

REINWAND:
The role of government is first to be the champion of the project. There is a lot of political value and capital created by launching these types of networks. Whether the driving force is political, from the IT side of stakeholder groups or the result of community activism, the municipality should build the excitement. Another thing they bring to the partnership is pole rights, the assets where you can mount the radios–the traffic signals, street lights. In some projects we've seen RFPs where it turns out the city doesn't have the rights to these assets. It doesn't add much value to the partnership if the vendor ultimately has to go and negotiate with the utilities or whomever owns the assets. The cities have a lot more leverage with the utilities than vendors do.

Governments need to endorse the service within the community because this really helps the Internet service provider drive their member acquisition costs down. You look at the brand equity of a city and you find that many citizens want to use the network services that the city offers, they have an affinity for those services.

On the vendor side, their responsibility is to identify the correct technology, install it, keep it in good working order. Service providers need to drive users to the network, and also be open to alternative business customers, not just the consumers. They need to look at applications such as automated meter reading. It's essential that a network operator keeps its options open.

NEWMAN:

The role of municipalities depends on their agenda. If they're looking for a public safety network such as Oklahoma City is, or a public works network such as you have in Corpus Christi for automated meter reading, it might make sense for local government to run everything. What we have seen to date is that larger cities then want to offer public access. Due to market pressures and the bandwidth demands for running a public access network it appears that this type of network is best run by private industry.

On the other hand, unless they are a suburb near a larger city, smaller cities and towns probably will need to build the network themselves as the capital markets have not fully embraced small private firms in this field yet.

BARTON:

You should structure a relationship that is mutually beneficial. On one hand, as a vendor, we're interested in selling as much product as we can. On the other, we're also in the business of making our customers happy—customers who are pleased with the return they get on their investment are the best evangelists a vendor can have.

The first step a community needs to take is to identify their needs and requirements. Obviously recommendations on network configuration differ depending upon the applications for which the network is to be used. For example, a network supporting public utilities plus mobile city government-worker use, but no public access, is configured differently than a network is to be used solely for public access to serve residences and small business. Clearly articulate what goals are critical so that vendors can do the best job of defining and designing a system to meet those needs.

Vendors need to understand that municipalities are not competitors with each other. With public organizations, things are much more collaborative. People who work in utilities or municipal departments tend to talk to peers in other cities. In this market it's very important that vendors have satisfied customers. If they do, other prospective customers will hear about it. And if they don't, prospective customers will hear about that too.

Building a broadband network is not a one-time transaction. There is any amount of post sales and post installation support. The conditions under which these networks operate are dynamic and can change over time, even season to season. There is a need for ongoing maintenance of network as well. We tend to remain in pretty close contact with customers even after the network is operational to make sure if performs to their satisfaction, and if it's not, to make the necessary adjustments. In addition, as city populations grow and neighborhoods expand, vendors need to continue working with the community on how best to expand their network within the city's architecture as seamlessly as possible.

BUTCHER:
Equal rewards and risks is the only way that this can work. It seems to me that with the cable roll out several years ago, the cities gave up their rights completely. They gave up their seat at the table to have a say in price, who gets it, where it goes. Right now they look at cable TV and see what they could have had.

This time with broadband the people who felt like they got burned want to make sure when they negotiate these deals that they get a seat at the table for the long term. They want a role in deciding who gets it, where it gets deployed, how much gets charged and how often the technology gets refreshed. Governments realize that they have valuable assets in these light posts and rooftops. They have leverage and they need to build into their contracts these leverage points. But communities also have to share in the risk somehow.

There are various ways to provide value. One is to alleviate the costs of mounting rights. It's like the farmer who negotiates a deal with a cellular carrier to receive payment to allow them to put a tower on his or her farm. Local government is in a position where they can put a fair market value to its assets and put that up in lieu of bonds or tax money. This way, both parties have a stake in the project's success and both will lose something if it fails.

DOLMETSCH:
Local governments have to promote the network effectively. Before rolling these things out, they need to come up with a marketing plan. Who's their target audience, what's the message for constituents? Is encouraging mobile commerce for local business the real initiative? Philly did a good job at promotions.

2. Can vendors with a financial interest in the outcome be objective partners in key municipality decisions?

REINWAND:

The most important thing to remember about the public and private sector is that one can't operate without the other. It's very symbiotic. The cities are the ones that have the poles and other key assets. The network operators bring their technical expertise, whatever hardware deals they've struck and so forth. Local governments that try to provide Internet services and customer support to end users on their own will eventually outsource these tasks back to the private sector. At the same time, network operators don't have those assets needed to physically deploy the network.

Everyone needs to be in a mutually beneficial partnership. Municipalities have their interests, whether it's social objectives such as closing the digital divide, giving mobile government workers wireless access to help them be more efficient, or even replacing expensive telecom infrastructure with a newer cheaper technology. These are the kinds of motivations we're seeing. If we can enable this at lower costs than otherwise available, then the cities are able to recognize a pretty good cost savings. That's why this is generating interest in both cities and the private sector.

BARTON:

This can be a double-edged sword. As I already mentioned, we want to sell so we obviously are going to put our best foot forward. However, if we don't think we can deliver a solution with which a customer is satisfied, we'll decline to bid. It's also the municipalities' responsibility to evaluate options objectively and be realistic in their expectations.

DOLMETSCH:

I think that sometimes vendors are not objective enough because they want to push products and technology. Whether that is providing too much infrastructure rather than thinking a little bit about of the best option, or trying to shoehorn a certain technology in where it doesn't fit. Maybe they don't consider the existing landline assets. If the local government does have fiber, then use it as backhaul. Look at a city's entire current infrastructure to weigh re-using it in some shape or form.

Sometimes the best way is to ensure objectivity is to hire consultant to identify your requirements. But to pick a good consultant, you probably should ask integrators for references. Integrators have been around longer than most broadband consultants providing general technology products and services to public safety as well as other government organizations. The consultant can then work with the systems integrator to evaluate vendor proposals.

3. What are some tips to government to help them work more effectively with vendors and service providers?

NEWMAN:
Understand the financial solvency of each service provider. Be aware that some vendors make claims about products that are not ready for market yet. If you're going to use the RFP process, make sure that the decision committee has good technical representation. It's advisable to bring in an experienced integrator, and make sure either you or they do the required homework on security requirements and processes.

There are some general things you can add to your checklist for creating the RFP. Document your government and stakeholder assets in advance. Offer anchor tenancy opportunities. Working with the local utility in advance of a RFP is critical if your municipality does not own the electric utility. Finally, have a first draft of the franchise agreement (or contract) completed in advance.

KHALIQ:
Before awarding the contract, one of the key values that governments should look at is whether that partner or vendor understands the government industry, as well as understands the broadband industry. Often when a government group looks at a major technology application, they need someone who has a more comprehensive view of how all parties can benefit. This is where a systems integrator such as IBM or a consultant can add value by bringing the necessary parties together to understand each other's needs.

You may get vendors that have a good grasp of issues regarding government or stakeholders' operations, but don't know what the issues and concerns are that pertain to the network. You have infrastructure, software applications different stakeholders plan to use, service provider issues, customer service concerns, etc. There are a lot of elements in a wide-area deployment. Each vendor can tell their piece of the story but not put it in the bigger context.

Once you begin deployment and during the implementation, the government needs to be partners all the way through as far as managing the process is concerned. But they're not in business to be a network operating center (NOC). Government would be better served to focus on what they're in the business for. Likewise vendors need to do what they're best at delivering.

BARTON:

After initial network deployment, its important to see who the actual users are among the government and various constituent groups. From our experience its more the rule than the exception that after deployment of the network for a specific set of applications and users, additional stakeholders seek to add access even though their requirements were not accounted for in the original plans. What seems like a simple change oftentimes changes the optimal equipment and design requirements.

So the main recommendation is get people to be clear up front about what they're planning to do on the network, or two bad things can happen. You can either commit to do a whole bunch of stuff that you end not doing, which means you deploy a lot more network than you need. Or, you under-scope the project and don't put in enough network or bandwidth, so availability does not meet expectations.

DOLMETSCH:

Make sure that the vendor or systems integrator has done this more than one time in their career. They need to understand the entire project. There are a whole lot of technology elements–security, switching and routing, bandwidth control. Though it's difficult in these early days of community broadband, it helps if whatever they've done has been operating for more than two years. Do they have proven statistics showing mean time to failure, system reliability, those types of things? Most of the vendors should have management systems that produce those stats and normally it's a requirement in the RFP.

Refer to archived RFPs for public safety applications to see their requirements. They usually ask for audited financial statements and balance sheets. The vendor can't be two people working out of a garage. Do vendor visits. We won a build for the city of Wichita, and the city sent people to our offices to make sure we were real before awarding the contract. Checking out references is very important.

As far as managing the project, after getting a contract vendors should put up a performance bond. The insurer that backs the bond guarantees that the application will work, and they can kick the vendor off a job and bring in someone else in if it doesn't work. If the vendor isn't a solid business, either they won't be able to get a bond or they'll have to pay a lot of money for one. Usually a vendor's viability to get a bond is uncovered during the RFP process.

During the project you should have weekly status meetings to say 'where are you, what is your progress.' There should be updated and documented network results and coverage maps.

4. Are there lines that vendors should not cross in their working in a public-private partnership?

BARTON:
Absolutely. There are obviously government officials who are held to tight ethical standards that are more stringent then you find in private industry in general. Vendors need to adhere to those standards, respect the purchasing process and not try to circumvent it. If you got an order that's going to be for 'x' amount of product and it's above a certain authorization, don't split that in two to try to hide the fact. Get the proper approvals–it will save a lot of headache and delays in the end.

Vendors have to respect 'Quiet periods' during the RFP process because if you're start lobbying during this period chances are pretty good you'll get thrown out. Or if you do get the business, you're going to raise a protest from other vendors that in the end delays the project.

An example is that Tropos had a city customer who had hosted a number of visits from prospective vendors. We wanted to take the group out to lunch. However there were a few restrictions…we could invite them to our facilities and share food brought in for our employees, but we couldn't take them out to a restaurant. This is just one example of the kinds of rules that as a vendor you need to respect and abide by.

REINWAND:
For many businesses it's always been standard practice to do everything by the book, and it's important that governments do this. They should always open the windows to an RFP or and RFI process. Ethical practices should be part of how every vendor does business. In communities where this is not the case, you're seeing a lot more crackdown on unethical activity. People are more aware of the ways that the rules can be bent, and they are intolerant about these infractions.

I like the local government setting strict requirements and then leaving an option for alternative proposals to be submitted. It's in interesting way to leave the door open by saying that 'we have strict requirements, but we're not opposed to hearing different ideas.' As part of the RFP process everyone has a chance to offer other options. That way, if the municipality accepts an alternative proposal, competitors can't say later they didn't have the opportunity to do the same thing.

As this technology evolves, there are lots of ways you're going to see of implementing broadband. While cities will be thinking one way today, two or three months down the road as bids start to come in, they may see something in an alternative proposal and say 'gee, I never thought of that. That's a fantastic idea.' You want to let the marketplace have that type of option as long as things are fair for everyone.

5. Can vendors get caught up in the politics of the government structure? How do you minimize the impact?

REINWAND:

The way to approach this is to make it very clear what the roles are for the city and for the network provider. When you draw the line clearly, it helps us avoid politics because we don't have to 'sell' the city on strategy. They understand what their needs are. Once you're operating, be sure to maintain clear expectations for the network. You can minimize concerns of council members if you work to establish specific performance criteria, have clear service level agreements, guarantees on remedies and defined lines of communication.

Communities that have been successful talked a lot about the benefits. I don't think any council member disagrees with the fact that broadband is going to help improve education, improve the lifestyle and so forth. A lot of their concerns are around how much this is going to cost. 'How are we going to make sure the provider does that what they say they're going to do?' Support the project champions in the communities by providing them with things that help address the vendor-responsibility issues with council members and other decision makers.

BARTON:

Part of this goes back to respecting the bid process. The bid process is supposed to somewhat remove the likelihood of political favoritism. The bigger issue is, someone such as a mayor or city council holds the purse strings, and someone in the city needs to champion the project who is close to these individuals. It's similar to a corporate sale where you need to understand where your power base is, who the influencers and decision makers are, and do everything you can to shore up your champion. However, a substantial difference is that a debate within a municipality about installing a network can get a lot of press and facilitate involvement from multiple parties.

You have to walk a line. There's a set of advocates you have to bring over to your side, there are some people on the fence who you're trying to convince to join your side and there are some people who are dead set against it and always will be. You're trying to find a way to neutralize this third group without making them a mortal enemy. It pays to be savvy in knowing how to navigate the politics, particularly when there's a lot of attention around the broadband project.

NEWMAN:

In a way, you can't get around the politics. But one way for vendors to minimize some of the hassles is to align with politicians who are on term limits because they're motivated to get things done before their terms are up. Democrats, Republicans, they're all the same. They understand that this broadband network brings economic development and it helps their communities be more competitive. So they'll take up the cause and be out front with it. The vendors can stay in the background.

DOLMETSCH:

Yes, vendors can get caught up in this. Normally the politics will be with a local carrier, or between different agencies within the government that don't agree. We normally mitigate this with contractual statements that say if there are delays due to the municipality or working with them, the community will have to bear the costs. We tell them that upfront. We respond to an RFP with certain assumptions and if there are any change orders, the client will pay. It does minimize these political issues dramatically. And we have not had a problem with government administration changes.

6. For vendors, do you expect there to be significant operational differences between delivering products and services to small versus large city governments?

DOLMETSCH:

No, it's not as far as physically putting up the network because even when you do a big city, it's broken up into chunks. You never look at this as one big picture. It really is a quilt, whether each part of the quilt is two square miles or 20 square miles. You have a grand plan, but it's always easier to bite it off into smaller pieces.

In smaller cities, the RFP process is a whole lot less political. For one thing, there are fewer politicians. Also, their budgeting process is much more defined. There is often one, maybe two decision makers. In a bigger city there may be 10.

REINWAND:

Working with the city and going through the RFP process is a time consuming and sales heavy process that requires a significant investment that you're hoping to spread out over a large market at some point. If it takes just as much time to work with a town of 1000 as it does with a city of 1 million, you probably prefer to work with a city that's larger.

You have great benefits in cities that are dense. If you look at a city like Miami Beach, there are a lot of people packed into a small area. Even though it's a small city, it's very attractive because the economics of how many people you can serve per radio goes way up.

With communities that are more spread out, you have to start looking at different type of technology. A mesh WiFi network with its typical access points isn't going to make economic sense when you can only cover three or four houses per square mile. The operational requirements are significantly different. You have to look at things such as fixed wireless. Provisioning is different. Professional installers have to come to the homes, climb up on the roof and mount the equipment. In order to get that installer there you have to schedule an appointment.

These operational complexities make the business model more challenging. This isn't to say that it can't be done. The economics are just on the verge of making it viable for companies to come in and address these issues.

BARTON:

As a matter of course, the larger the program, the more complex and more difficult it is to manage and the more carefully it has to be managed. When you're working with larger cities the visibility is higher, and the media-level politicking is much higher.

When looking at vendors, the size of cities in which they have deployed and their expertise in the technology are interrelated in some ways, but scalability is still a big issue. Some vendors' systems are inherently more scalable allowing them to roll out across broader coverage areas. When you have technology that allows you to flexibly scale to a larger city, then you're more likely to have success. Smaller cities can work with less robust technology, but as those cities develop and expand over time, the less robust technology decision can result in a dead-end and an expensive infrastructure upgrade.

In the end, the goals of a city are more important than the size of the community. If all they want to do is light up a hot zone around a sports complex or community center, then this is less technically challenging than rolling out to 10 square miles. There are fewer vendors whose products can work effectively in a 10 square-mile area then in a network covering a few blocks.

CHAPTER 10

Broadband Deployment Management Issues

A professional project manager could probably write a book just on the topic of managing broadband implementations. There are lots of issues to address, potential headaches and heartburn to avoid, unforeseeable challenges to overcome and opportunities to seize that can only come with sound project management. However, this level of detail will have to wait for my next book.

This chapter gives you a general list of people-management tasks, a few insights on managing expectations, a more detailed look at keeping network security in perspective and a summary guide on marketing your broadband services. This last item might raise a few eyebrows, but it shouldn't. Even if the private sector company is totally in charge of the network, any government that wants the broadband network in their community to impact economic development, digital inclusion, et al must be prepared to manage an effective campaign to market the network.

Managing People

Trying to get the most productivity and creativity from workers involved with technology deployments, especially volunteers, leans more toward mysticism than defined science for the next year or so until best practices become widely agreed upon. Expect a certain amount of trial and error. In the meantime here are some easy guidelines you should find helpful. Feel free to add suggestions via my blog or Twitter.

1. Know everyone's limitation.

Broadband is hip, happening and sexy now that it's in the news all the time, so quite a few people want to be in on the action. But on both the business side and the IT side, you have to resist the personal or political pressure to put people in administrative positions of responsibility on the project team unless the positions match their capabilities and availability. Likewise, you have to keep higher-ups and pseudo-techies from directly controlling or influencing deployment processes for which they have little expertise.

IT people already overworked with projects don't need day-to-day programming and network testing responsibilities for a new broadband application added to their plate. Rely on the vendor or systems integrator for this. Business managers who haven't been directly involved in a major technology deployment in 10 years shouldn't be writing the technical requirements to give to IT–at least not alone. Appoint someone to guide your deployment who has the ability, resolve and authority to make the right human resource assignments, to remove or re-assign key people if they're not cutting it and to take projects outside of the organization if necessary.

2. Put someone in charge who knows the technology–or is willing to learn.

Relatively few managers, executives and even IT people are experts in broadband. They don't need to be. But they do need to develop a working knowledge of the technology, be aggressive about asking questions of IT pros, vendors, consultants, etc. and not have ego issues with saying "I don't know."

3. Don't undervalue end users' feedback.

One of the skills executives and project managers need to sharpen is their ability to effective solicit and properly act on end user feedback. Several people have commented on how they get maximum user acceptance of technology applications by responding to feedback early in the process. And failing to get ahead of the curve, at least instigate that feedback the minute you sense a problem brewing with your deployment. The good manager knows that often the solution is not on their boss' desk, but in their customers' (subscribers') hands.

4. Minimize the role of those who manage too much or too little.

Once you kick the network deployment into motion, particularly one that involves many hundreds of miles and numerous stakeholders, there are people and materiel logistics involved to rival the Normandy D-Day invasion. This is the time to scoot those project team members you discover to be micro managers over to some other tasks, or maybe onto the steering committee.

People who need to have their hands on every little detail or set up 101 approval processes and inadvertent pitfalls threaten to slow down the overall project, or prevent those who know their job best from getting it done. In the current economy it should be fairly easy to retain professional project managers on a temporary basis after the needs assessment to ensure things get done properly, but without having the emotional attachment that leads to micro managing.

Conversely, you can't afford to have absentee managers calling the shots. Greg Lush of the Linc Group, a global technical building services firm, lets his people do their thing, but he will step in if the project starts to miss deadlines or stray from the plan. You need people who can find that middle road between too much and too little control that best fits your situation, preferably before the project starts rather than after. The pilot project gives you an opportunity to assess where your team member's personalities fit on the control spectrum.

Managing Expectations—A Never-Ending Job

The demon/angel that hovers in the wings of every deployment performance is Expectation. When reality intersects or misses Expectation–of deadlines, budgets, ROI, network benefits, productivity, technology limitations, etc–you either have heavenly bliss or hell on wheels. Here are a couple tips to help you have more of the former than the latter.

1. Whatever you think, double it or cut it by a third.

When dealing with relatively young technology such as community broadband, assume that everything takes twice as long and costs twice as much, and often the results expected from the technology will be less than what you eventually get. There can be as many reasons for this as there are organizations. But nevertheless, bad things happen during deployment when someone important who expects or needs the project to cost "x" or be finished by "y" and produce "z" is disappointed with what they really get. Remember, no company ever went out of business and few people have ever been fired for a project that finished ahead of the expected schedule and under promised budget.

2. Skepticism in appropriate doses is good for the bottom line.

Salespeople have one primary mission, which is to sell things, though keeping the customer satisfied is hopefully a close second. And more times than the industry likes to admit, salespeople don't know a lot about the technology they're selling. So, until you become thoroughly convinced that the sales reps before you have your best interests at heart and a better-than-passing technical knowledge of their product, be relentless in determining if their products are likely to perform as planned. A previous vendor burned Tom Kilcourse, Director of Facilities Management for The Ratner Group, which owns the national chain of Hair Cuttery salons. So he went to the next vendor's offices to meet with their top executives in person and took his IT director with him.

Granted, the pilot is supposed to uncover issues such as this, but there are so many different technology dynamics at play in large deployments that you never know how an application is really going to scale until you get in the middle of one. So do yourself a favor and insist that vendors have contingency plans for possible problems as well as a guarantee they'll resolve any problems. Being the skeptic, don't assume they plan to bear this cost. Ask. With multi-vendor projects, expect finger pointing if any major breakdowns happen. If you can, develop some service agreement language that protects you in this scenario.

3. Be honest about what vendors should expect from your organization.

Vendors' salespeople are not always at fault when organizations end up with networks and applications that don't perform as advertised. When an organization doesn't clearly articulate what they want or expect, or the pilot doesn't adequately uncover what their mobile workers expect, then communities often get poor results. If the vendors expect, based on what you tell them, that you have perfectly running business operations, that's what they'll build to. However, if your communication procedures are in dire need of improving, then the application you get probably isn't going to produce the results you need.

It has happened that some stakeholders don't like to talk in too much detail about their inner business workings for security reasons, which is understandable. But you should make a decision about how you're going to deal with the potential of getting network results that are less than what you or stakeholders demand because they don't want to give vendors the details necessary to build what they need.

4. Be prepared for Murphy's Law of Unintended Consequences.

Murphy's Law says that what can go wrong will go wrong. His Law of Untended Consequences of Technology is, sometimes so much can go right that things go wrong. One group was successful in reaching their wireless application's goal of reducing the need for truck drivers, but they soon started having an unexpected loyalty and retention challenge with the ones who were left. Another company increased the efficiency so much for their field workers that shortcomings in the home office operations suddenly had to be addressed.

Communities expect some success, but without proper expectations set, they could be in as much trouble as those who don't have contingency plans in case the network under-performs. This is something local governments should pay close attention to since mobile workers using the network can re-define the roles of those desk-bound staffers inside City Hall. Stakeholders may even slow their network adoption so they can adjust.

You need to plan for change before you start the pilot process. But even so, when an application does what it's supposed to at a city- or countywide level, you could be surprised when floodgates to ideas for new applications burst open. Oklahoma City and New York City both launched massive city-use only wireless networks specifically to address one or two applications. However, they soon had to structure formal submission procedures for ideas and an internal planning/prioritization mechanism for those ideas because people started expecting the project team to make new applications available immediately.

Take advantage of early successes

It pays to take advantage of–and heavily promote–early successes so you make more bearable the challenge of balancing expectations that constituents create on their own with the realities of network deployment schedules. This gives you a little breathing room and maintains high-level support during the time it takes to finish deployment AND see some of the major benefits. Some benefits might be immediately apparent, while it can be many months for other benefits to be quantifiable.

1. Know what the business manager's hot button issues are–promote them first.

You may be ecstatic that the new servers allow 500 mobile government users on the network to simultaneously access the time card application. The city departments' senior administrators' first concern, however, is that the old system required eight steps to complete log-in procedures, and this killed time that workers could have been inspecting business sites. Are the new servers going to eliminate most of these steps? If you want to keep the network's budget healthy, start every meeting talking about how quickly people can log-in.

2. Don't underestimate the little things.

Stakeholders often care most about the smallest technology benefits. The big picture of broadband's potential impact may motivate your IT people on the project team. But the largest business customer on the network may swoon over the ability to be able to run a videoconference with its warehouse managers across town. So as you set up the pilot project or begin deployment, make sure that customer gets the capability they want first (if practical). They won't be able to stop singing your praises while you pursue the big dream.

3. Everything is a potential early success to be promoted.

Hardware distributed on time, workers trained ahead of schedule, an increase in data that's captured on network servers. Success at every level is positive PR, for keeping both the project team and stakeholders excited and engaged in the project. Just don't overdo it. A weekly update during the first couple of months of deployment that lists two or three simple advances that the average non-techie can understand should be fine.

4. Create an early warning system.

As eagerly as you want to claim bragging rights for early successes, you also want to nip complaints about the network in the bud. The pilot process should uncover and address most of the issues that can cause stakeholders or general subscribers to become disgruntled. Yet expect somebody somewhere will get a burr under their saddle about something. During the first stage of deployment have a feedback mechanism of some sort linking network users directly to the project team so you uncover, acknowledge and quickly respond to any complaints. Don't let one vocal individual incite a chain reaction.

5. Paint a picture of great glories.

After accumulating a series of initial successes, show senior administrators how these initial successes are the foundation for greater benefits that will make yours a leader among municipal or county governments. Being a leader stokes the community's collective ego. This ego equity becomes valuable political equity for the team when you're eight months into a year-long deployment, some of the greater payoffs are still a ways off, and a new election might replace some of the officials who championed the project. But if you're producing clear wins early and can tap into visionaries' long-term thinking, you'll do well getting over the deployment's middle stages.

Managing Security—Boogieman of the Under-Informed, Handmaiden of the Obstructionist

"A lot of security consultants scare the crap out of people. And sure, if you do things wrong, security breeches will happen. A dedicated hacker can get in. But really, how often is that going to happen? Worry enough–lock your door, set the alarm. But you don't need barb wire and machine gun turrets." Bill Brook, former Director, of Information Technology Chicago's Children's Memorial Hospital, sums up the security management discussion pretty well.

Managing the discussion of security early on is vital because it's at the heart of a lot of resistance to community broadband, particularly wireless, both from within the community and from those whose interests are adversely affected by muni networks. Within communities you find those who want to restrict WiFi networks to government use only, and those who want no other applications running on a wireless network except public safety are the ones vigorously waving the security flag. I ran a workshop once for community stakeholders where the two public safety guys walked out partway through, refusing even to listen to the idea of sharing "their" network.

The folks outside of communities who play the security card a lot are the giant telcos and cable companies. For the last five years I've listened to representatives of telecommunications industry associations deride the value of muni wireless, stating that no emergency first responders would rely on WiFi because of the "lack of security." The next time you hear people throw these arguments out, relate the following wireless security success story to them.

Morrow County, where security failure isn't an option

In Morrow County, Oregon you will find the Umatilla Chemical Depot that holds about one-third of the U.S. remaining stockpile of warfare materials. This county is home to the Hanford Nuclear Reservation. They also operate a nuclear power station. One of the major east-west rail lines in the western U.S. runs through this county. Morrow County hosts major natural gas and energy production and distribution facilities. Talk about a hot spot!

The Morrow County Emergency Management Center's (MCEMC) team of first responders relies on a 1000-square mile WiFi network to manage a myriad of monitoring and emergency response resources prepared for a potential nightmare of a catastrophe. And yet no one loses one night's sleep over security of the network. Your city should send every critic of WiFi security to spend 15 minutes in Morrow County. While you're at it, send the directors of your emergency response teams out there to see some of the interesting Homeland Security-funded initiatives they have in place.

Cameras linked to the network are streaming real-time, full-speed color video to monitor all of these facilities, and they can be remotely controlled to turn and zoom in on specific areas. The same type of cameras monitors the highways since in the event of a chemical disaster the staff has about 10 minutes in which to respond. If they need to quickly evacuate residents, MCEMC relies on those cameras and the network to remotely re-direct traffic by controlling traffic lights, drop arm barriers and billboard-size message signs that can post new text as needed (FEMA, are you listening?).

MCEMC deployed WiFi access points mounted on buoys on the rivers and waterways to provide warnings to watercraft as well as back up to land-based WiFi points. This same system can operate un-manned fire boats to fight hazardous materials fires on or near shores. The main PBX phone lines all have VoIP capability that also provides backups to the cell phones.

Emergency response vehicles are equipped with mobile WiFi access points so they can stay connected to the network while driving up to 100 mph. The network is HIPAA-certified safe so that patient data can be wirelessly transmitted while en route to hospitals. On top of that, the network is also Fed Info Protection Standard (FIPS 140-2). Passing muster for both of these intensely high levels of security is equivalent to parting the Red Sea and walking on water. All of this sort of begs the question, why is it MCEMC doesn't worry very much about security being breached, or network failure at a critical time?

Putting security into perspective

When MCEMC Director Casey Beard was an Intelligence officer for the U.S. Army, someone in the military went into hyper-security mode because it was possible, with the right equipment, to monitor a person's PC keystrokes in order to figure out passwords and such. "So we had all of these lead shields brought in for the walls, PCs were put inside special metal boxes and so on," Beard states.

"Then one day I was thinking about it and realized that, sure, you could intercept keystrokes. But you'd need a lab environment to do it, which would require a semi trailer full of high tech gear and a bunch of antennas on the outside and it would have to be parked almost in front of the building. Something like that sitting outside would be pretty obvious, I think. Historically with technology, the threats are often greater than the reality."

Casey believes that any network is as strong as its weakest point, so his team works at keeping the weak spots strong. They bought a couple of commercially available WiFi security applications to provide the HIPAA and FIPS security, and later hired a security team to come in with special equipment to try to hack the network, which they couldn't do. They constantly follow all of the standard security practices such as hounding employees to secure passwords, not link into access points without the appropriate security features enabled on their devices, etc.

"There's always going to be a tradeoff between being able to use information versus protecting it. If you want total security, then don't use technology at all."

To address the issue of what happens when natural disaster strikes, Casey's crew relies on not one, but two massive fiber networks that come in all the way from Portland. The WiFi mesh integrates with the fiber networks and also has the access points densely deployed so as to provide overlapping coverage over many areas.

There are trickle charge batteries that back these up for eight-to-twelve hours and in some case solar panels recharge the batteries, plus uninterrupted power supplies and standard generators provide yet more backup. The access points are placed to minimize vandalism. Don't forget about those mobile access points for yet another level of redundancy. If all else fails, Casey tells me they keep an adequate supply of white boards and grease pens.

Telecom industry reps and other anti muni broadband people for a while were fond of saying that WiFi isn't more reliable than any other communication option, citing the effects Hurricane Katrina which caused all of the communication structure in New Orleans to collapse. This is true. But the day following the worst of the storm's impact, the mayor managed to get in touch with the world by going down to an office supply store and borrowing some WiFi equipment.

WiFi might have collapsed along with everything else, but it was also one of the first things to come back online. Roving teams of volunteers in various parts of the devastated areas brought in WiFi equipment and VoIP gear to connect displaced relatives with their loved ones. Even when cell phone calls weren't getting through, text messages were moving in and out.

Knocking down the Boogieman

Believing that boogiemen and obstructionists should be cast from our midst, here are some tips on how you can make good security decisions and move on. At the fringe of the network where access point meets computing device, security is in the hands of the subscribers as much as it is when that person's using a computer with a wireline connection. It is possible and advisable, though, to give the user more tools for security than are commonly available on wireline connections.

Conversely, if a municipality's or any stakeholders' Web and intranet servers are adequately secured, are they are no more vulnerable to hacking from someone with WiFi access than someone on a landline. Using your home as an analogy, once you secure your house (including the top floors) from every type of illegal access, it doesn't matter much if burglars walk to your front door, take a cab or drop out of the sky. You're safe. If you don't secure your servers and access points or monitor effectively for rogue access points, then bad things will happen. I realize that finding a hacker may be harder if they use an access point, but that's another issue.

The average citizen is going to going to be a weak point in their own security picture as long as they don't enact safety precautions on their computers and mobile devices, which you can encourage but probably shouldn't legislate. The potential is pretty high for laws enforcing personal safety precautions to do more harm than good.

Address security and get on with the business at hand

A network security team that's part of the Lee County Port Authority's IT group identifies what security areas they want to address and let their service provider implement the system to those specs. A pilot system is configured to those specifics, installed and then tested by a third party that validates everything, identifies anomalies and makes recommendations.

The Authority's staff makes additions, changes, deletes and alterations to the systems after provider installs them, receives training by the provider, and acts as the first line of support. Security analysts from Cisco, SBC and Siemens perform hacking drills once or twice a year, and the staff adopts analysts' suggested fixes for any vulnerabilities. They vary the firms doing the security tests to keep the process free of preconceived concepts.

Robert Smallback, Jr., the Authority's Senior IS Manager, states, "recently our wireless application was tested by the local TV investigative reporter who hired two hackers to challenge our site. The report was excellent, showing that our wireless network was very robust and easy to use. They could get into wireless devices used by transit system passengers but the hackers rarely could see the Port Authority's network. And when they did, they couldn't penetrate it. If we had developed the system in-house, and configured it for security, then tested it ourselves, we would not have gained the value of the service providers' expertise. You can do it once the best that you can, or you can turn the job over to people who do it for their daily bread. I'd go with the experts."

Security is indeed a serious matter. But as Brook concludes, "We're following all best practices. If you have confidence that you can secure your network, then you will be comfortable. But there are CIOs who are not technical, or CFOs who've seen these Tom Cruise Mission Impossible movies, so they fear the worst." Don't let the Boogie Man cloud your decisions.

Don't Forget Your Marketing Campaign

Though it may not be top of mind when you begin that long day's journey into broadband, marketing of the network is the cornerstone of your business plan. Marketing begins long before the network goes live, during your pilot projects at the very least. Subsequently, one of your management tasks has to be executing a marketing plan.

The broadband stimulus program has spawned an interesting term–sustainable broadband adoption. Though I don't think there's anyplace where Congress or the Federal agencies directly involved in broadband have officially defined the term, everyone involved throws it around continually. Plain old broadband adoption is simply people subscribing to your service. Sustainable in one sense means you have to keep people using broadband, particularly people whose economic status you wish to raise through their active use of the Internet.

I look at sustainable broadband adoption (SAB) in an additional context. This network you're planning to build, it has to be sustained financially or else all of your dreams of community change facilitated by broadband goes up in smoke. Since hoping for grants and loans to keep the network afloat is a tenuous business strategy at best, the only way you're going to sustain it is by generating an endless stream of paying customers. "Paying" is the watchword.

Marketing is how you get those paying subscribers through the door, and it's what keeps them coming back year after year. Marketing is a never-ending process for as long as you hope to sustain the network. Furthermore, if one of you ultimate goals is to get low-income people on the network and keep them there, marketing is still necessary. That's because frankly, my dear, many low-income individuals don't give a damn about the Internet even if the service is free. My grandmother, were she alive, would tell you that if it's free they definitely won't see a value.

Here are a few high-level guidelines for waging your campaign for the hearts, minds and checkbooks of those whose support can ensure your network's financial success. This campaign plays to the 80-20 rule, meaning reaching that 20% of your potential subscriber base that will generate 80% of your direct broadband revenue.

Marketing to local government

Town, city and county governments should be your lead anchor tenants. They have clear identifiable communication needs, such as overhauling old, expensive technology, mobile workforce automation and improved community interaction that can represent tens if not hundreds of thousands of dollars in savings and revenue. This needs to be the thrust of your marketing message to this audience. The ability to run public safety and other applications that make the network eligible for grant assistance from state or federal agencies is the secondary marketing message.

The actual marketing campaign is going to be more along the lines of direct sales. Get face time with the right people, lay out the business case, go for the close. To prepare, get a platoon of foot soldiers (IT or city manager staffs are likely recruit pools) going door-to-door to the various city or county government departments during the needs assessment process to pose key fact-finding questions.

Some of your questions to department managers are: what are you spending for voice or data communications, if your proposed network can replace this existing infrastructure, what are the cost savings; if you're planning a wireless network (or anticipate adding it to the fiber network later); what mobile workforce applications can you introduce and for what cost savings; what government services can be delivered more effectively over the network, and at what cost savings; how would public safety be improved, and what will this mean in cost reductions and grant appeal.

Pull out your calculators and spreadsheets, do the math, make the numbers the centerpiece of your presentation and work your magic. If you've made a strong case, you should be able to sign up at least a couple of departments. Remember Oklahoma City and New York. One or two high-profile applications proving good return on investment will have other departments knocking on your door. Once the network is built, the cost to sustain government adoption is the price of sneaker equity and word-of-mouth publicity as you stay in touch with people advocating for greater use of the network.

Marketing to your local business community

The business community, as a block, is probably your second best source of anchor tenants, what I also refer to as institutional customers. Many communities typically have a handful of companies that need super highspeed broadband access. This is also a target audience one-on-one selling. If you create an extra strong financial foundation for the network, convince these businesses to become investors in the network appealing whose fees for premium highspeed service plus a percentage above buys them a stake in the network's success. The pitch was simple. It would cost less for each business to collectively fund the network then separately get incumbents to bring similar services to each business.

Next you have the general midsize and small companies that need access. They typically are willing to pay more than individual subscription rates for premium services, though these likely don't need to be the same speeds as your largest subscribers. Expect to do a fair amount of direct marketing to promote your broadband services, such as mailings, brochures and radio ads. But you also need to budget for workshops and other types of educational activities to get businesses up to speed on how they can use broadband. The less businesses have been exposed to Net access, the steeper the learning curve and resulting costs for education.

Home based businesses make up the third area where you can drive adoption, though to predict how much revenue this could be you have to survey your constituents. Marketing to this group may be most effective if done through community groups, nonprofits and local colleges that cater to adults and seniors likely to be looking for supplemental income or something to hold them over while they're unemployed. Those who are entrepreneurial by nature or who have worked for larger companies and are starting businesses at home are pre-disposed to using the Internet, so they will be at your doorstep the day the network goes live.

Finally, consider creating a marketing effort to use the network as a major draw for several large businesses to move to your area. For example, Lafayette, LA was negotiating with a call center operation to move there bringing 600 jobs. The head of the public utility that is driving the network project used the promise of the city's fiber network to help close the deal. This effort should piggyback on top of whatever the local chamber of commerce and economic development agency is doing to promote your community.

Marketing to the medical and healthcare community

The medical community offers you the opportunity to drive adoption two ways. First by being institutional customers. Second, through the hospitals and medical centers using the network to engage constituents and deliver services, thus driving up residential network subscribers.

When done correctly, the needs assessment process uncovers the hot-button issues that will motivate the medical community to subscribe to broadband services. Sending digital images and other high bandwidth data to doctors' offices or hospitals in other cities, replacing old data communication infrastructure, enhancing voice services, creating emergency backup communication systems are a few.

Your medical community stakeholders who help you during the needs assessment probably have a vision for using broadband to transform healthcare delivery in your community. These are the best people to spearhead your marketing drive since personal marketing is key for the medical community. To give their marketing efforts greater persuasive power, make time to research grant sources that may underwrite the healthcare applications your champion envisions.

To cast the medical community as drivers of residential and even small business adoption, sell them on the idea of making preventative healthcare content available on the network. They can post information such as healthy eating tips, how to detect warning signs of particular illnesses, etc. The aggressiveness with which healthcare facilities want to pursue this type of activity to pull constituents to their content determines how much they drive residential adoption and resulting revenue. Try to get the hospital to pick up some of the marketing costs for outreach to residents and local government or other organizations can match the rest.

CHAPTER 11

TCO—the Stealth Threat to a Successful Deployment

In discussions about broadband deployments, you hear a lot about ROI–return on investment. Why it's important, how to calculate it, why it's difficult for communities to measure it since so much of what they want to achieve with their networks is not about generating direct revenues. What often escapes attention in the discussion about ROI within all industries, not just government, is TCO–total cost of ownership.

I read a tweet (Twitter message) recently that said "the 'I' in ROI = the total cost of ownership." TCO is everything that it costs you to buy, deploy and manage the network during the life of its operation, which is more than the price of infrastructure hardware, network management software and consulting services. How much of a return you get or don't get from your network is directly affected by TCO, which can be a nasty surprise if you don't make plans to keep TCO under control. An example of un-anticipated costs is the time and money expense of dealing with obscure city or state ordinances and right of way laws that some don't think about researching in the excitement of launching the project.

One reason TCO catches people unaware is that there aren't a lot of broadband deployments fully completed, or enough best practices established so we have standard metrics for what various elements of the buildout should cost. The size of projects and the variety of network types (middle mile, last mile, WiFi, fiber etc.) are all over the map, further complicating the ability to predict TCO. Fortunately, there are some steps you can take to manage these expenses. This chapter tackles several main contributors to TCO.

While there's no formula for calculating TCO, there are general issues to consider and questions to ask within the organization and of the vendors you use. The objective is to identify a series of line items beyond obvious costs that should be factored into the budget and budget management. This requires extensive feedback gathering to find out what's needed to make the technology fully functional for network users–training, upgrades, replacement parts, big incumbents' legal attacks, customer support and so on. You also need to thoroughly research where technology capabilities and feature sets are headed so you don't pay a surprise cost for product obsolescence.

Don't let this discussion slow you down, just become wiser for it. It will help you anticipate, adapt and respond.

Should We Standardize or Use Proprietary Systems?

The question of standards applies across the board for deploying all the various flavors of broadband. It comes down to do you buy infrastructure components that 1) all conform to one industry standard, 2) conform to a variety of industry standards or 3) come from vendors that use their own proprietary standards?

For example, though there are different versions of it, WiFi is a prevalent standard for wireless networks. This is one reason there was immediate nationwide interest in building these networks in 2006. Not only did network radio transmitters (access points) from several vendors use this standard, hundreds of millions of mobile devices, laptops and other products used by potential subscribers supported WiFi. It seemed the whole technology world was supporting one industry standard. Cities and stakeholders didn't have to worry about spending extra money to equip workers with special mobile devices. Most could use devices they already had to immediately jump onto the network.

However, you must be careful you don't standardize on the wrong technology. If WiFi is the wrong technology to standardize on for your particular network needs, then you'll soon see your TCO skyrocket.

Standardization impacts TCO in a couple of important ways. The greater the volume of products manufactured that meet a standard, the less they cost due to economies of scale in production. Demand drives prices down. Outdoor network access points that cost $5,000 in 2007 may cost half that amount now. This could reduce your overall network costs by a third or more from what a completed network would have cost two or three years ago.

Often the cost of maintaining the network is also less with standardized technology. Joe Savage, President of the Fiber to the Home Council, states that the standard for fiber has become so common and dependable that "people don't bother pilot testing fiber networks, they just connect everything up and turn it on. They're not worried about things such as firewalls and network monitoring software, it's all standard now." When Athens, GA built its network before WiFi outdoor access points were introduced, the equipment they used was kluged together components from different sources. When something malfunctioned, a lot of hours were spent repairing the problem because they couldn't call up a retailer to get a replacement unit.

Staff related costs are less to support products that conform to one standard because IT doesn't have to learn or "hire in" different skills sets, or stockpile large quantities of replacement parts. Also, when particular infrastructure products become the standard, there are more software and development tools available which support them, so there's less of a need for custom software development, another major staff expense. Finally, if a vendor with a proprietary standard goes out of business, you won't be able to easily get support, upgrades or replacement parts when something goes wrong.

Infrastructure bought today that doesn't support common standards may not work well with technology you buy two years from now, causing communication breakdowns. And many cities have found that the proprietary wireless networks they own for public safety are islands of technology that can't easily be integrated with new technology, or used by those coming from outside of the community such as federal agencies.

Explore all your options

Decisions need to be made about standards for all aspects of the broadband equation. With the broadband network, the main question you want to ask infrastructure and application vendors is, which standards do they support and what is the life expectancy of the standards. Then go talk to industry experts to have them assess vendor responses.

Rizwan Khaliq of IBM believes that industry standardization is going to be a big benefit to communities. "You want to look at how well these standards are going to be 'future proof' or scaleable. On the network side, you have WiMAX and the like that are still being tested. On the embedded technology side, you have standards that are going to become increasingly important when you want to do things such as use the network to remotely monitor bridges or machine operations at chemical plants."

That said, some cities have found success while going against the norm. Providence, R.I.'s network has been going strong since 2006. A small company with proprietary technology built it, though the deal was sealed only after Motorola bought them, which alleviated worries about the small vendor going out of business. The network is based on IP technology, so in that respect Providence did go with a standard, but the main infrastructure isn't WiFi. Grand Rapids, MI settled on Wi MAX from Clearwire for their citywide network before the provider had any other installations up.

In both cases only government workers use the networks. Because the subscriber base is small, specialized and controlled by the respective cities, walking down the non-standards path required extra soul-searching but in the end it wasn't viewed as a serious risk. They did a thorough needs analysis and technology evaluation, and determined any additional costs that might come from workers needing add-in cards for laptops or other extras were justified based on potential benefits. There's a lot to think about, yet in the end your community may decide to make a similar decision.

Avoiding the TCO Impact of Obsolescence

A frequent TCO concern is technology obsolescence. If communities don't plan properly for the frequent fadeout of one technology and the introduction of a new, improved technology, there can be financial hell to pay.

WiFi continues to be a solid bet because aspects of the technology have become more powerful for outdoor use, particularly products built to the new (for now) 802.11n standard. The incredibly popular Apple iPhone with its WiFi capability is driving legions of other smart-phones and even some cell phones to build in WiFi capabilities, which gives you a bigger pool of potential subscribers anxious to find WiFi networks beyond hotspots. This pent up demand means you can spend a little less in marketing and still attract customers.

Elements of broadband are evolving, but fiber is constantly touted as "future proof" because once it is installed, it keeps going and going without much danger of becoming obsolete. If WiMAX continues being deployed another year through 2010, which definitely could be the case given the potential number of WiMAX projects to receive broadband stimulus funding, this technology will become a safer bet.

These technologies reflect only part of the obsolescence discussion, and even with these you have the need to be constantly vigilant to developments that can affect the length of their lifecycle. The stimulus program could open the door for new categories of wireless technology to take hold or new variations of commonly used wireless such as WiFi that may become the "in thing" within a year or two. Market-savvy vendors, of course, can help ensure their future technology is backward compatible to their products you buy today. But you can't rely on them to cover your assets.

Proper previous planning saves the day

"Put your money on the technology that's in the computing device," advises Intel's Paul Butcher. "Bet on technology that's deployed to millions of people. I think you look at the handset or the device that's walking around with the greatest number of people, and build infrastructure behind that technology." This is valid for some aspects of broadband, but networks that connect inanimate objects such as smart utility meters for smart grid applications require different thinking. As 2010 begins, most of the smart meter manufacturers are small companies, and many of them have proprietary technology rather than support for IP or WiFi. The danger of obsolescence is quite prevalent here.

Besides the potential obsolescence of a technology category or technology standards, you face the issue of individual vendors' products becoming out of date. Broadband deployments require multiple vendors and ISPs whose respective pieces of the technology puzzle evolve at different speeds. Require in the RFP that the winning company upgrades the network as technologies change. This not only gets the service provider and vendors to underwrite the effort, thus removing the expense from your TCO, but also forces them and you to plan technology roadmaps for their products or services.

If the project team is a little uncertain about their ability to manage this process effectively, designate a prime contractor or system integrator. The Arizona Government Information Technology Agency received a grant to map broadband in the state, and one of the steps they took was to hire a contractor who's responsible for reviewing all vendors the agency uses. If can be helpful to have an expert on an on-going basis who advises you on the potential lifecycle of a new technology and how it can be successfully integrated into the network.

One view I've subscribed to for a long time is that you shouldn't plan to replace an entire infrastructure or particular product just because it's old, as long as new components you add are backward compatible with your original equipment. And as long as the older equipment still performs the way you need it to.

On the blog site Muniwireless.com, my column about Philadelphia buying and upgrading the network EarthLink built in 2007 sparked a lively debate about whether that equipment is obsolete. Brian Webster, formerly with EarthLink as the Chief RF Engineer on the Philly project, wrote, "the existing Tropos radios can deliver 6 megs to an end user as they are installed now. If there is extensive use of fiber to backhaul the traffic, performance should be maintained. I have not worked with any of the upgraded Tropos firmware, but I have no reason to believe that it won't perform even better." Avoid throwing the baby out with the bathwater.

You also shouldn't plan to immediately jump on the "next big thing." Even though technology changes rapidly, people often over estimate the pace at which new technology will be adopted–if it is adopted at all. In 1999 I worked for Metricom, which marketed the Ricochet Internet access service, the precursor to today's municipal wireless networks. All of us at the company and many journalists who wrote about it swore Richochet service was the imminent future of American urban life. The company failed miserably, in part because it was ahead of its time. The history of technology is full of stories such as this. As long as a technology continues to support the apps that you want to use, it's not obsolete. Serve the base that's out there now rather than what might be adopted in the future.

Vendors have a role

When you're reviewing vendors, take into account whether they have people on staff monitoring technology changes. If so, they should be familiar with negotiating the dangers of obsolescence. On your end, understand current and future requirements of the network and the applications stakeholders want to run on the. Agree to have regular meetings with your vendors' soothsayers so you're not blindsided by negative technology developments.

One question that might come to mind is, what do you do if you get into the middle of an implementation, or maybe a couple of years down the road, and realize you haven't budgeted properly for obsolescence? This will result in spending a lot of money up front and more later for an expensive upgrade later.

The best way to avoid a network mid-life crisis is for the project team and stakeholders to do a lot of forward thinking all the time. What are possible future developments such as new RFID, sudden population increases, public safety applications such as GPS tracking of missing kids, or greater business demand for online video conferencing? How do we build the network today so that it's ready if someone has to come in and add greater backhaul capacity, new spectrum or technology that's going to provide a different type of infrastructure? Can our IT people support these changes and also ensure that the vendor can support the changes as well?

It is the vendors' role, especially in it's response to an RFP, to offer flexible solutions as well as point out the shortcomings in an RFP. You won't be able to respond to future developments if you box yourself into a corner from the very beginning.

Dolmetsch concludes that "if they don't see certain things in an RFP, vendors should say 'you really need to be thinking about this. This is what it's really going to cost to add this kind of support later. You don't want to go in there and just throw up a barebones system.' Typically when we respond to RFPs and we find items aren't included in there that should be, we insert them as options along with explanations about why what we're proposing is a better solution."

Ultimately the best vendors and service providers to select are those known to be reputable and are willing to evolve your application through a long-term relationship. This type of supplier sits down with you to develop a growth plan and help estimate the up-front costs, then proceeds with a pilot program so you can run tests to see if the network performs as advertised.

Look behind the curtains...

Conduct vigorous research to determine not only if vendors and service providers' people, products and services but also their finances are up to the challenge of making your network successful. Are these entities likely to be around for a while? For a vendor to effectively analyze and respond to changes in the technology, the market and your community while still providing you with proper service, they need ample staff and funds. It still amazes me how many cities failed to do the simple math after news stories about muni network builder MetroFi's financial standing, and figure out there was no way the network company could deliver the broadband they promised.

Once you find vendors that can supply what you're looking for, talk to their customers who are implementing (or have implemented) similar projects as you to get feedback on the pros and cons on the vendors' products as well as the quality and responsiveness of their customer service.

Whether your government organization is large or small, there are some benefits of going with smaller vendors to meet some of your technology requirements, though this tends to run counter to the cautious nature of some IT people. With small companies you often get more attention from people who will work closely with you to provide the right solution because your contract is worth more to their growth than vendors that have hundreds of customers.

Be leery of a lot of forward pitching from large vendors, meaning they tell you "yes, we can do everything you want" but fail to mention that it will be a year later when version 3.0 ships before they can do it. Find out what's usable now and see how it can evolve over the next five years. How will it dovetail into new broadband technology that you might buy later?

Prepare for occasional partnership strains

Organizations may not care so much about the size of vendors or service providers as they do the quality of customer service and support that's offered. If the products and the companies do what's advertised and their post-sales support meets their pre-sales advertising, then this should be a mutually beneficial relationship.

Since you need to mix and match applications and technology to meet diverse broadband needs, you obviously get the best possible solutions when you do this effectively. However, you have contingency plans for the downside of resolving technical problems. Due to complexity of integrated technology, finding the source of problems is difficult if vendors can't sort themselves out because no one really wants to take responsibility for the problem, which TCO can spike upward. Put good service contracts in place to protect you from this issue.

Contingency planning also should address vendor bankruptcy or acquisition, even if they are solid as a rock when you first engage them. I don't think you can bank on everyone being here in three years, at least not under their present form and ownership. The exception may be the lead companies in projects funded with broadband stimulus money. If they take this federal money they can't sell or merge the business for 10 years. I'm not sure what will happen when reality meets regulation, but here at least you may have some assurance these companies will be around for a reasonable time.

Create a backup plan for all the other vendors and providers so you have a quick response and minimal grief and aggravation in case one of them isn't there when you wake up one morning. Some vendors don't fail, they just get swallowed up by bigger companies. Then you have to worry about questions such as what if the quality of service slips, or the new owners won't support the products you already bought.

It is common for large organizations to require developers of critical software applications to keep copies of the software code in escrow so the customer can get it in case of bankruptcy or acquisition. You should consider something similar for the broadband assets you purchase. Some of the wiser municipalities signed contracts with the companies running citywide wireless networks that allow the government to take over the asset in case the company failed and ensure that broadband services continue. Plan for the best, and also plan for the worse. You can't go wrong.

Some General TCO Management Tips

I advised that you minimize both TCO and management headaches if you appoint, hire or sub-contract someone or a company to deal with the various vendors and service providers as a way to address obsolescence. But they can also alleviate a few important business management issues. On-going planning, overseeing technology compatibility testing, enforcing project delivery times and handling billing are some of the business functions in which potential hidden costs are multiplied manifold when you work with different providers simultaneously.

Having a good contractor does a lot to remove the headaches of managing multiple vendor relationships, but you still need someone inside your organization who has an active role in this process. Otherwise you risk losing control of the deployment project, and increase the odds that vendors will not be kept abreast of changes within the organization and among stakeholders that can impact the use of these applications.

One sure way to reduce TCO is learn how others resolve problems before they occur. Tom Baumgartner of the Pinellas County Sheriff's Office describes steps they used to contain costs for managing their departmental WiFi network. "On the IT side, we implemented a centralized managing system that monitors and updates access points at any given time. IT could resolve problems quickly and efficiently by checking alerts on the management system. We also created a feature to alert departments' managers if their people aren't adhering to policy."

If your project team is running the network, have your vendor add network management features that regularly check operations status of key infrastructure components, detect if anything is about to fail, try to re-start failed equipment and so on. Ideally, your network management software will automatically create documentation and a schematic as assets are added or removed from the network. It can be extremely time consuming a year or two down the road to do maintenance and upgrades if you or new people on the project team can't find half your assets.

Be prepared for change management. New technology that significantly alters the way people work demands that you adequately prepare to deal with the resulting changes or face possible operational struggles that eat up time, cause subscriber defections and otherwise negate some or all of the anticipated benefits of broadband. For example, local governments that shift data access to the field can lead to increased decision-making by mobile workers not accustomed to this role. If you don't spend time preparing them for this new responsibility, they could make bad decisions that are costly.

Though it's expensive to buy and keep spare equipment in storage, it costs a lot in subscriber loyalty, their productivity loss and increased customer support calls when you can't repair network failures quickly enough. To keep TCO manageable, frequently conduct analysis to keep just the right amount of equipment on hand.

An access point failing in a densely packed urban area with multiple access points per block probably won't be noticeable right away. But networks in sparsely populated suburban and rural areas have a greater reliance on each transmitter. Plan accordingly. If your area is subject to major natural disasters, you may want to keep a back up equipment supply in quantities that can replace the sudden loss of 15%–25% of your network infrastructure.

One last thing to keep in mind about TCO. It's a direct spawn of Murphy's Law. If technology deployments can cost more, take longer to complete and uncover the unexpected, they will. Your best defense is proper previous planning, followed by a good pilot project, and insured by perpetual vigilance.

Peeling Back the TCO of Two Broadband Operations

I want to briefly explore two areas of operation and associated TCO issues that result from the overhead of delivering services to network subscribes: customer service and digital inclusion programs. Both operations can catch you by surprise with higher than expected costs because they are very labor intensive to execute properly, with digital inclusion perhaps being harder to control because few best practices are in place. Customer service is an area where TCO can significantly increase if you become more successful than anticipated. Customer service for network subscribers is definitely one area that a municipality should have its public utility, private partners or an outside contracted group run.

Doug Berman is Principle Consultant for Data Security at the firm Zofii. Prior to this he was in customer service for 15 years helping customers deploy small and large broadband networks. From his experience, "clearly the highest costs are people related. The number of staff you need depends on many details, size of the network being the top of the list. The larger the network, both in physical size and subscriber base, the more resources you'll likely require. Costs are also heavily dependent on the type of applications the network supports for various stakeholders. Will your customer service center be open 9:00-to-5:00 or 24/7? The latter increases your costs exponentially."

There are a many other costs that can potentially creep up on you. Will you need to rent office space or can you merge your network customer service with your public utility's support team? Expenses for power, phones, call tracking systems, desks, cubes, laptops, servers, bucket trucks, and a laboratory to test and reproduce customer issues need to be estimated based low, average and high subscriber numbers. All of these factors will require research on what fits best for your budget and environment.

Communities in areas with dramatically different seasons find these changes impact the volume and cost of trips to service the infrastructure, for example. Extreme temperatures can cause infrastructure components to malfunction more often. Make sure you are aware of ordinances that can impact infrastructure support. In one market where Berman's former company built a network, they were required to use union labor, which significantly raised the costs of deploying radios.

When launching a broadband project, don't forget the link between the quality of the service (QOS) vendors provide to you, and how much you spend supporting the network and subscribers. "Some vendors tend to exaggerate on a range of topics," warns Berman. "Be sure they set proper expectations about the number of transmitters required, for example or the maturity of software features so you minimize hidden TCO." It costs time and money to send people and trucks out on a second run to add additional infrastructure. If you have to wait hours for a vendor to fix a problem, your service resources and future sales could sag under the weight of irate subscribers.

When you establish pricing for service contracts for subscribers, particularly your institutional customers, don't overlook the cost of hardware and software warranties along with technical support from all of your vendors. There are a lot of moving parts here, given the variety of vendors, the different technology requirements of respective stakeholders, the number of municipalities if it's a regional project, etc. Network construction, subscriber sales and finance operations all need to be joined at the hip together with project management to ensure costs are accurately estimated, contracts are properly negotiated and pricing policies don't create TCO booby traps.

The real cost of digital inclusion

Remember the digital divide? In 2006 it was the face of public policy that launched a thousand municipal wireless projects. Using broadband to attack the digital divide, though now we use the politically acceptable term "digital inclusion," isn't so much a discussion about infrastructure as it is about a complex coordinated collection of community service activities. However, I'm addressing it here in the TCO chapter because 1) it is a major broadband initiative for many communities, and 2) it carries great potential for sticker shock once you get into the program.

One of the reasons communities wanted municipal wireless to be free originally was so they could provide access for low-income constituents and others who otherwise wouldn't be able to access the Internet. Let's be clear about one thing. Digital inclusion isn't free. It isn't even cheap!

Those who pursued digital inclusion quickly discovered that the TCO goes far beyond the cost of building and supporting a network for users who may not become paying customers for some time. Besides subsidizing Internet access, you need training and hardware for constituents who may not be able to afford either. But this is just the half of it.

A useful digital inclusion effort for even a moderate-size population (200,000–300,000) is a major business operation requiring staff and money. Riverside, CA and Philadelphia set up nonprofit corporations, which they highly recommend doing to minimize bureaucratic entanglements and maximize effectiveness. This means upfront costs to create the entity that can come to between $200,000 and a million dollars depending on the size of the city and other factors.

Expect annual operating costs that equal 50% of your startup costs. The nonprofit organization requires a management team and staff, office facilities and all the usual accoutrements. They have to raise money for running the office and the programs they create. Fundraising costs money.

There needs to be a marketing campaign (or lots of knocking on doors) to entice organizations to denote the hardware, and a lot of logistical coordination to receive and store them. What's more, you can't just take in computers at an empty storefront and then re-distribute them. You have to refurbish the units first, which takes longer than some think. If you want people from underserved areas to do the work so you keep money flowing within these communities, you have to recruit, train, manage and pay them. If the populations are chronically unemployed and have had limited exposure to technology, you have to work harder and more hours to create an efficient workforce.

Then there's the extra effort to distribute hardware and serve constituents who are hard to reach, a challenge to train and whose success adopting and using the technology is not easy to track. Smart Riverside and Digital Impact Group have waged the equivalent of trench warfare to partner with dozens of nonprofits that help target and deliver the technology and training. It's painstaking work serving 100 people here, 70 people there.

Digital Impact Group CEO Greg Goldman believes "you cannot have a meaningful digital inclusion program unless it addresses all four of the main barriers to underserved communities participating in the digital economy: complexity, cost, literacy and experience. You must resolve all four issues." If digital inclusion is a major goal for your community and stakeholders, then your budget should reflect that you understand the total money and time costs related to executing a serious program.

To Sum It Up

Figuring out ahead of time what your total cost of ownership is going to be 50% analytics, 50% crystal ball gazing as it pertains to the broadband network. However you approach the mechanics of the task, it is important that you allow for more of everything. More time, more money, more headaches, more odds and ends. Don't go overboard, of course, but give yourself some room for Murphy's Law.

Press everyone you work with inside and outside of the project team to take a second and third look at all of the factors that drive costs. Local government organizations of all types are great at exchanging experiences and ideas among peers. Use this to your advantage and find out what other agencies and their community stakeholders are doing, what expenses they're encountering and how they are keeping costs contained. Go to your business communities that have deployed wireless applications and see how they have managed TCO.

TCO must not be an afterthought. That said, do not let people use TCO as an excuse to delay moving forward. "How do we know such and such won't cost more than estimated?" is a valid question. But as Robert Bright says, "sometimes you just can't tell what's going to happen until you move forward." Put someone in charge of monitoring deployments for those factors that can increase costs–delays, equipment breakage, financial news, political activities, etc. As they spot something significant, make adjustments and move forward.

CHAPTER 12

The ROI at the End of the Rainbow

Do you run broadband networks the same as you do a typical public works project or more similar to a business endeavor? And for those advocating the latter, do you comprehend what a completely different mindset this requires compared to how public administrators approach purely government projects?

In my 2006 book on muni wireless, I argued that local governments have to think like a business if they want to build, or partner with the private sector to build, a network that generates enough revenues and cost savings to sustain network operations. Following this logic, developing a return on investment (ROI) analysis is one of the main disciplines that result from this new mindset.

If you intend for the network buildout and operations to be run entirely by a private company, you still should vet their ROI process. Companies may squawk at the "intrusion," but as I mentioned last chapter, a close probe of MetroFi would have led a lot of cities to steer clear because there was no ROI case for the company after they accumulated six or seven project wins. Without a clear and credible (emphasis on "credible") plan to achieve ROI for your specific network, it will fail and your constituents still won't have broadband. Several cities have endured two or three financial failures by private-sector owners of their networks that obviously didn't plan well enough.

Getting a Handle on Your ROI

There are some differences in how community broadband produces an ROI compared to commercial projects that have fairly clear lines to profits and losses. For one thing, some of the returns to the community may be difficult or impossible to quantify, such as improving quality-of-life issues. Other benefits, such as assisting the delivery of telemedicine services, may be facilitated through the efforts of several constituencies and stakeholder groups. With different sources and factors contributing to success, it's hard to attribute some benefits directly to broadband.

Regardless the differences between public and commercial entities, broadband ROI goals need to be set, along with specific metrics by which you can evaluate some of the changes produced after the network is operating for a while. Public administrators and project teams are capable of adopting a business mindset for network projects, but they may have to re-assign someone from outside the group or hire an expert to establish ROI objectives and an on-going analysis process. Possibly this person can return a year or so after the network launches to audit ROI findings.

Wilson, NC gets ahead of the ROI curve

I frequently reference Wilson, NC because 1) Time Warner Cable (TWC) repeatedly tried to shaft that state's muni network efforts through legislative shenanigans–and failed, and 2) the town is ahead of their ROI schedule while delivering better service for less money. Wilson sells residents a 10-megabits per seconds (Mbps) service for a third less than TWC, a 100 Mbps service that TWC doesn't even have and a 1-gigabit per second service for organizations that's off the hook. One reason they're doing so well is because they aren't rushing their ROI.

Unlike large commercial entities that seem to be governed by the quarterly P & L, Wilson is working on a 12-year ROI payback. "Uptown Services, a municipal broadband consulting firm, did a feasibility study for us before we expanded the network," states Brian Bowman, City of Wilson's Public Affairs Manager. "We had already built a fiber ring to our facilities. They predicted we'd be cash flow positive if we reached 30% penetration within three full years. Their data also said the network would be paid off after about 12 years if we reached that figure. We presented the findings to City Council, and they voted unanimously to move forward with expansion."

A year and a half into the business, Greenlight (the Wilson broadband services' name) is over halfway to their first major milestone, with 21.4% market penetration. The analysis appears to be accurate if a little on the conservative side, which to me is the sign of a good analysis. If you don't have people on staff who can conduct the type of analysis you need, don't be shy about going outside of your organization or community to find the expertise.

The bottom line here is, try not to put undo pressure on your team to produce great ROI results at lightning speed. As a private entity, 12 years may be unrealistic. However, if you're trying to turn-n-burn to earn a quick buck, maybe community broadband isn't the venture you should be in at this time.

Take note, Wilson's revenue comes entirely from subscribers. "Council was very careful to avoid the use of tax money," states Bowman. "Our city's largest employer, BB&T, was one of our first paying customers and has been a great supporter of Greenlight. Wilson Community College and Barton College are also on board." Remember to strengthen your ROI case by bringing institutional customers onboard early.

Don't ignore the need to create a viable contingency plan in case revenues start to fall short of projections. Wilson didn't have much choice in writing a backup plan. They had to get the blessing of the NC Local Government Commission, an independent group that decides whether local governments in the state should borrow money for specific projects based on their plans. "We had to include a contingency plan to get their blessing on our application for $28 million in bank loans," recalls Bowman. "If memory serves, we committed to either a 1.4% increase in our electric rates, or an increase in taxes of 5 cents per $100 valuation on property to make up for missing our ROI numbers. We haven't had to use either method and don't expect to."

Full-Frontal Business Thinking

When I say governments and nonprofits need to think as if they were business operations, I don't mean just for the purpose of commissioning analysis work. You need to examine the entire broadband buildout and operations process with the same critical eye as a cynical entrepreneur, but without losing site of the fact you have to serve the public good through this project's success.

Michael Johnston is VP of IT and Broadband at Jackson Energy Authority, a public utility in Tennessee. The City of Jackson has a population of 75,000. Their fiber network is currently a success story with 16,000 subscribers, but it had a rocky start. Johnston gives a blunt assessment of why "you need to do a gut check before you go after broadband. You can't be nice fluffy business person."

Whether you write a proposal to get broadband stimulus and other government grant money, or write a standard business plan to help secure traditional commercial funding, you have to show how you can financially sustain the network after it's built. What's your ROI under normal, best case, or worst case scenarios?

"Let's say we just borrowed $10 million with the assumption we'll get 100 new subscribers every month for a year," states Johnston. "But what about the price of greater success? If you get 200 subscribers a month, what do you do? You need more customer service people, more technicians. Beating your 'take plan' is counterproductive if you can't get any more 'free' government money and you have to go to the bank for real money." In this respect, the business of broadband is as much about managing growth as curtailing losses.

The challenge of public-private partnerships

I often comment on the value of partnering, the staple of any business venture and a factor in your eventual ROI. With community stakeholders, these partners are likely to be on the same page as you in terms of what they want. But the public/private partnership that has become a community broadband orthodoxy, the Holy Grail if you will, also can be the source of great heartburn.

"Partnering with a telco does help because you have to be ready for the different world of telecom operations. The difficulty however, is that regardless of what size telco you partner with, you can have completely different goals that are at cross-purposes. The city wants to deliver services in places where it's currently not offered. The partner needs to make money. There's a reason that partner isn't already delivering service in your area."

Though sometimes easier said than done, I suggest you spend a lot of time in frank conversation so both parties thoroughly understand how the other's business works. Such a discussion opens your eyes to where potential troubles lie that could lead to irreconcilable differences.

Construct and evaluate your business model with clear knowledge of how it relates to partners. UTOPIA, the municipal network in Utah, took on debt via a bond and couldn't (by law) provide anything but the Internet pipe. This has been a typical middle mile project scenario. Service providers connect to the pipe to build last mile infrastructure that delivers services directly to consumers. UTOPIA makes money on fees from providers based on how many of their customers use the network.

"This kind of arrangement should be a winner, but it doesn't always work. 'My plan says if the provider adds 100 customers/month, the total amount of fees from the provider that I get for those 100 subscribers pays off the monthly bond debt.' But what if the partner doesn't add that many customers. The city has no leverage because private partners want the least number of customers to ensure the most profit. Acquiring more customers costs money that cuts into profits. If the city insists on getting their fee anyway for 100 customers, the partner leaves. So obviously the city can't raise fees."

Johnston makes a goods point about reconciling the respective ROI needs of the public and nonprofit partners and the commercial partners. It's interesting to note that the agencies awarding stimulus grants structured the rules to encourage applicants for middle mile networks to form partnerships with institutions such as schools and hospitals. This generates revenues to offset the potential scenario that Johnston describes.

The Intelligent Community Forum (ICF) is a think tank that studies the economic and social development of the 21st Century community. They annually give communities across the world special recognition for leadership in making their citizens' lives better, with broadband often playing a major role in this accomplishment. ICF sees a lot of the inner workings of broadband projects.

ICF co-founder Robert Bell believes you can work past conflicting financial objectives of public and private partners. "It is important for the private and public sides of a partnership to enter the deal with their eyes wide open. Private companies want to gain access to markets; governments want to gain access to expertise and the assets of the provider. When the assets remain in the carrier's control or ownership, this leaves the ROI issues with the carrier. That's a clean line of demarcation. Where a partnership creates shared assets by the public and private sector partners, things get more complicated and both sides need to work out a wide range of issues well in advance."

The challenge of consumer subscribers

Johnston points to a particular ROI-influencer that every community broadband project team needs to consider regardless of which entity or partnership is running the network. The concept that adding more customers does not necessarily result in greater profit is probably counterintuitive to many. However, this impact on ROI is one big reason why you don't have broadband access in both urban and rural communities, and an issue you must address if you are to make credible ROI forecasts.

Galen Updike, Telecommunications Development Manager at the State of Arizona's Government Information Technology Agency (GITA), makes an interesting point. "It's extremely difficult for private sector companies to financially benefit from many of broadband's economic development benefits to communities," Galen says, "because these do not directly impact companies' bottom line. Therefore, communities have to spend a lot of time with potential partners working on this puzzle, or else face failure by the private partner in the long run."

Does adding more customers cut into profit? Depends on the type of customer. Due to the cost-to-revenue equation, individual consumer customers are a huge money-sink, and thus a challenging market to tap for a profitable revenue stream.

An examination of some current subscription rates in the Minneapolis wireless market reveals the reality of revenue. US Internet charges individuals about $20/month for a rate of 1 to 6 Mbps downstream, while Clearwire charges $25/month for 1 Mbps downstream up to $45/mo for 3 to 6 Mbps downstream for unlimited use. Though the specific speeds customers receive vary, this $25–$50 range of prices hold true for basic services in rural (where broadband exists) as well as urban areas.

A service provider has little latitude to raise the basic rates before people refuse to buy, so many of them abandon or avoid certain markets altogether in favor of areas where they have some leeway to raise prices. But it is the cost of winning, servicing and managing individual subscribers that causes providers to limit the number of these customers within a service area.

According to former Verizon executives Tom Terry and Tony Unitas of Terry & Unitas Associates, a technology and business consulting firm, "it costs $100 or more in marketing and sales support to win a residential customer, and about 20% of this amount for marketing to retain customers.

At $25/month in subscription revenues, it takes four months to recover customer acquisition costs and many months more to catch up with customer retention costs. What's more, service and support costs can easily outstrip revenue, particularly in areas where people have little or no prior experience with the Internet. Handling one call to resolve a browser or Internet security issue can easily erase two or three months of revenue. That's not profit, mind you, that's total revenue received from the subscriber.

By and large, community broadband cannot rely on individual subscribers alone to create a financially sustainable business model because there's no profit there. Oklahoma City, OK and Seattle, WA are two cities that believe it's better to give wireless services away for free because of the customer support costs required for paying customers. So how does the broadband team plan to make a profit? The answer rests with the local businesses.

The average business customer is willing to pay more for the same service a consumer buys, plus buy more expensive services that consumers typically won't, such as 1 gigabit per second Internet access. Furthermore, businesses are less likely to change providers because doing so significantly disrupts their operations and potentially their cash flow.

Vince Jordan, President of RidgeviewTel (a Successful.com business partner), has been in telecommunications for over 20 years. He found that, "dollar for dollar it costs 20 times more to manage and maintain an individual customer than a business customer. With 50 individuals, we'll get 50 calls with service questions, complaints, etc. With a business of 50 employees, we're only going to get one call to solve 50 people's problem.

"In terms of revenue and profitability, having a business customer with 50 employees is the similar to having 350 – 400 individual subscribers. If the Federal government didn't mandate they sign on individual customers, the telecom industry would have abandoned consumers decades ago because you can't charge them enough."

So the bottom line here is simple. If you plan to create a financially sustainable network, particularly in communities where maybe 90% of the potential customers for broadband are residential, you must create a viable strategy to move the cost-to-revenue equation in your favor.

Additional ROI Planning Tactics

Simply stated, the quest for the best ROI revolves around generating as much quantifiable revenue as possible, while controlling spending for network operations as much as possible without sacrificing service quality. The tricky

John Dolmetsch has been involved with a million square miles of municipal deployment of one type of wireless infrastructure or another. He points right away to the low hanging fruit in terms of making the ROI case.

In most areas of the country there's a significant cost justification to deploy these networks outside of generating Internet access subscribers. Some cities' ROI model could justify the investment in broadband within 24 months through its impact on replacing the recurring fees they're paying for inter-building connectivity such as T1 lines.

"If you look at a typical city, they could probably cost justify building a network just to connect its own schools and government buildings, achieving ROI somewhere between 18 and 36 months. I haven't seen one city yet where that's not the case. Typically when we go into an area and start dealing with a government, the first thing we tell them is to go back and add up all their current costs for connecting buildings and users within those buildings."

His is a variation on my premise that the cost-savings and revenue-generating benefits of broadband wireless for mobile government workers can justify whatever else you do with the network. Eliminating recurring costs lays the groundwork for the rest of the infrastructure. To use a Dolmetsch analogy, "you build main highway routes through your area. Once these are in place, building the sides streets to individual businesses and other organizations are nowhere near as expensive." By thus lowering the buildout expense for reaching subscribers who pay for premium services, you structure a better ROI model.

Bell goes a step further and suggests that you use the savings to expand the network into other communities. "Some small rural communities have been able to extend their networks into neighboring municipalities and counties, becoming the telecom and IT service provider of choice across a wide area." The winds of opportunity blow in your favor for such a move, assuming you act quickly and logically, and there aren't restrictive muni network laws such as there are in Tennessee and Utah.

To achieve this expansion, "local governments typically set up their own CLECs or lodge responsibility for the network in a city-owned utility or similar entity," continues Bell. "These organizations invest more like businesses, meaning a larger risk on buildout and higher expectations for ROI, which goes into the municipality's general fund. They hire IT and telecom professionals to run the businesses and motivate them to meet the business plan."

A new take on middle mile

Of the handful of broadband stimulus grants that have been awarded, most go to middle mile projects. But unlike UTOPIA with its restrictions on direct sales to subscribers, these grant awardees each appears to target 200-300 institutions for direct service sales. This strategy is good since it gives you a source of premium revenues while leaving business and costly-to-acquire consumer prospects to last-mile providers. As a middle mile network owner with the ability to sell to institutions, you won't be as vulnerable to last-mile providers with different ROI needs.

Any direct-to-subscriber sales strategy depends on effective service pricing to succeed. The school district wants to be a customer, for example. You want to ensure all citizens the best education. So you offer the district broadband that's 10 times faster at a price 70% lower than the incumbent's bid. Perhaps you can do this and still cover network operating costs. Should you? Heavens no! Don't gouge them, but institutional customers expect–and budget–to pay more for premium services that delivers better value. Trust me, one day you'll need the money. And you won't upset your partners.

ROI Projection Is Not All About Revenue Generation

Part of the answer to the question "How do we get our money's worth from broadband?" is determined by dollars earned or saved, time saved, an increase in tasks performed with the same number of staff and other quantifiables. However, project teams and stakeholders eventually have to face the fact that the network produces intangible benefits that make a formulaic approach to analyzing ROI inappropriate at times.

"Are you trying to maximize profits and city dollars?" Bright asks. "That's part of equation, but that's not the whole equation. You can't put a price on increasing school education levels of the population, on improving access to continuing educational opportunities. It's very difficult to put an absolute number on many things a community does, part of this dollar goes here, part of that dollar goes there. It's not like a standard ROI model for a business. We as a community must step back and recognize this when we're talking about what services to offer, how we price it. Sometimes, you can't use a micrometer to measure every advance and say you're going to maximize every facet of it because you'll never get the job done."

You can decide how the intangible benefits of the network can be evaluated to determine an acceptable ROI through the consensus-building and expectation management recommended in previous chapters. Accept that there are shades grey in the value that broadband delivers, though this isn't always bad. Benefits that were unforeseen at the start of the project can appear if you probe deeply enough to find them. Or conversely, some of the promised ROI falls short of expectations because of factors beyond project teams' control. The bottom line is that the business of governments is to deliver or facilitate community benefits on which it's difficult or impossible to set a price.

The ROI of anticipating expenses

While the amount of ROI you generate is determined a lot by the benefits your network produces, your expenses for building and operating the network also significantly contribute to or detract from your return. Chapter 11 focused specifically on managing the TCO of the equation, and covers a lot of valuable ground, but there's always the question how do you budget for those unknown costs? Look to the engineering planning phase for one answer. How well you assess stakeholders' needs determines the cost effectiveness of your engineering design, which in turn helps you develop a more accurate budget.

If your community has a shipping port area where wireless will support a small number of workers and asset management tasks that don't transmit a lot of data, you don't need to overpopulate this area with access points. But if the network has to support an area with hundreds of users per square block or 60 businesses needing gigabytes per second of data, you'll need a higher density of access points and a lot of fiber.

Knowing where not to spend too much while avoiding under-builds in other areas that you have to correct later affects ROI. But you have to be realistic about the fact that you can't foretell some dramatic changes, such as neighborhood revitalization working so well you have four times as many users per square block. So maybe the solution is having your engineering firm design network infrastructure or buy network management software that allows for those changes. You control or prevent future budget spikes by "over-building" strategic components of the network.

For communities that initially plan a limited initial downtown deployment or a single-use application such as for managing utility meters, but may expand the network later, consider over-building the NOC. The NOC is an expensive element of the buildout initially, but when built properly the same facility can drive a square-mile network now and a 50 square-mile network later. Putting more capacity into the back office for the short term better controls your budget in the long run.

Does your engineering design maximize the cost-containment value of asset re-utilization? For example, did the technology inventory you created during the needs assessment reveal lit or dark fiber? If so, consider a plan that allows you to tap existing excess capacity as the source of support for new network services to sell so you can open new business opportunities without incurring new costs.

Also, rather than build a network operating center (NOC), which is expensive for delivering business-grade service since you need people working there 24/7, can your public utility's call center operation take on the role of a NOC. Thus you control a potentially expensive budget item by assigning it to a group more qualified to project and manage costs for that particular expense.

Whether you use license and unlicensed spectrum for wireless broadband has a budget impact. WiFi is unlicensed spectrum and it doesn't cost anything to use. But its broadcast power limitations means you have to install a lot of access points, though new technology is reducing this limitation. Conversely WiMAX is a cost saver in rural areas because its data transmission covers wide areas between radio transmitters, but WiMAX is a licensed spectrum that you have to buy and it's not necessarily cheap.

The real budget buster, though, is if you run out of licensed spectrum because the population increases significantly and either there's no more left to buy, or a large incumbent outbids you for what's available. As much as you can control aspects of your network infrastructure and services, there are outside forces beyond your control.

The net of all this is, the business (read: finance) side of the house cannot remove itself from discussions with engineering design firms and tech experts. Much of what these techies do has a profound impact on your ability to control or project developments impact your budget, so stay engaged with tem before and after the network is built to ensure a better ROI.

Marketing decisions affect costs...

Does your business plan reflect the future competitive landscape? What, you think that incumbents won't jump in just because they initially refused to build a network in your community? Put your business hat back on! That competition is going to impact your ROI.

"People are assuming their competitors are going to stand still. They think 'we're going to go in and take 60% of the market.' If you take that 60%, the competition doesn't sit there and say 'oh well.' They fight back. They send out mailers telling your subscribers 'I'll give you free cable for a year, Mr/Ms Muni Customer, if you just come back.' Municipalities have to match these kinds of offers or lose customers, and typically governments don't think about this."

This brings us to the battle of churn. Either you, if you're building a last-mile network, or the service provider using your middle mile have to address the fact that general consumers are inclined to switch broadband services at the drop of a hat. You have a couple of options. One is to play this game, but that requires an aggressive marketing mindset and sizeable monetary resources.

From years of marketing experience, I recommend not getting into that expensive trench warfare of brochures, ads and cut-throat price reductions in a never-ending race to the lowest possible price. Big companies can drain your bank account and come out on top. I suggest creating services that incumbents can't easily match, or can't match at all for several years, and sell them to institutional customers and businesses at premium prices.

However, if you do decide to play in churning waters, your ROI analysis has to account for extra marketing, sales and customer service investments to generate returns that could vary wildly from month to month. CPEs are one example of what can happen to your ROI when technology components become marketing pawns.

Because wireless data transmissions have trouble penetrating walls, almost every subscriber needs a CPE to get the best coverage. With no competition, there's less incentive to bundle this with subscribers' services at no extra charge. But once competitors come to town, the pressure to lower prices and give away goodies becomes great. Public and private organizations not used to competition can make what seem like great marketing decisions, such as using tech gear or certain data services to entice customers, which are really bad for short- and long-term ROI.

Marketing decisions cannot be made in a vacuum when it comes to broadband. Sales negotiations can lead to promises that require new infrastructure buildouts. Promotional campaigns can produce too many customers for the network to handle (think AT&T and the iPhone affect). Engineering, Customer Support, Finance and Marketing need to be at the planning table before decisions with potentially big consequences are made.

Preparing to Track ROI

Evaluating the broadband network's ROI is a challenge given that much of the benefits a community derives from the infrastructure depends on how stakeholders and constituent groups use it. One major step in making the task easier to measure infrastructure and applications ROI is coordinating with these groups to establish ROI objectives before the pilot, then review these right after the pilots. Try to get consensus on 1) whether the objectives to be measured are realistic, and 2) should the ROI objectives be more clearly defined. Each institutional customer and stakeholder group should have criteria specific to them as well for measuring ROI.

When I look at the objectives cities present in their RFPs, most are easy to comprehend, ambitious, noble and inspire support. But are they realistic for the specific communities? Does a city have the resources, and more importantly do they have the will, to undertake and complete the post-deployment work that's required to get the job done? Do these objectives have enough specific details so everyone unequivocally knows when it is they have achieved something worthwhile? If everyone's on shaky ground here, what is it exactly you're measuring for success later?

Assessing ROI where the rubber meets the road

For local governments wanting to gage their improvement communicating with citizens, constituent Internet portals can be built with analysis tools to measure how much of what content is being pushed out to, or accessed by constituents. These plus internal analyses can quantify the impact of the network on cities' communication and marketing budgets. Web analysis and traditional survey tools can tell you what services citizens and visitors are receiving through the network and their level of satisfaction so you can measure its impact on your service delivery operation.

There are various ways for stakeholders to measure improvements in their internal operations once the network launches, starting with how much they're saving by eliminating recurring telecommunication service charges. If they wireless-enable many of their assets in addition to their workforces, for example, the cost-savings and equipment performance enhancement due to improved asset maintenance alone can be a real eye-opener within a year or so.

Set up basic achievement milestones (e.g. subscribers added, parking meter revenue increased) for three, six and nine months following the network's launch, and see how well you reach or surpass these milestones. It not only builds your political capital for other broadband initiatives when stakeholders are successful, but if they're not quite making the numbers for one quarter, they can make mid-course adjustments. Since large metropolitan and county networks are deployed in segments, you can start tracking results for neighborhoods as they come online, though the full ROI likely won't come until the entire network is up and running.

You may need to set up feedback-gathering systems that mainly assess anecdotal evidence of success. Paul Larsen of Brigham City, UT states, "much of the information we have is anecdotal, based on direct feedback from individuals and companies whose needs previously were not being met. One individual now using the network prefers to work from home because he is more efficient and gets more done. An acquaintance is paying to bring fiber to the office where she works because she gets monthly recurring cost savings that will provide an ROI within a few months.

"There are many other such stories that reinforce our belief this infrastructure is changing our community for the better. We haven't spent a lot of time discussing benchmarks, perhaps because benchmarks have been set individually in the minds of everyone who worked on bringing the network here."

In the final analysis...

How often you report your ROI details depends on your particular circumstances. You might want do quarterly reporting if the political heat opposing the initiative was high, or there is a high level of general community interest in the outcome. Otherwise, semi-annual or annual reporting should be fine. Internally, though, monitor these numbers like a hawk during the first year. Keep your vendors appraised in case technical factors are influencing ROI.

Here are some general tips to help you evaluate how far you've come. 1) Focus on one or two of the most important benefits the application can deliver, and then look carefully at how well those benefits were delivered. 2) During ROI analysis, actively search for the unplanned benefits since these could be more beneficial to an organization than the original reasons for buying the application. 3) Open everyone's mind to explore the future benefits once constituents get comfortable and truly proficient with the technology.

The "narrow-focus" ROI

The "single purpose in being" approach for measuring ROI has merit. You can look at Scottsburg, Indiana, for example, says Jeff Arnold from the National Association of Counties. "They've done a great job. They were able to keep three plants that are main sources of jobs in that area because they spent almost $300,000 to set up a strong wireless network. But they had that single critical motivator. The companies said 'either we have broadband connectivity or we're out of here.' That was the incentive for Scottsburg to move forward instantly and try to find a solution that made sense. The broadband solution for them certainly was the way to go in terms of community benefits relative to the costs."

If you have a manufacturing plant or a wheat processing facility that needs high speed connectivity, then the benefits to the community of improving their business operations plus the resulting increase of tax revenues might prove to be sufficient ROI. Along with their main objective, Scottsburg also created a business model in which they specified what turned out to be an obtainable number of paid subscriptions to sell in the first year to further offset the investment.

This focus on one or two main objectives can be the easiest and fastest analysis to do, but be realistic in how much dollar value you place on some benefits. A few project teams end up spending more time on this than is necessary, such as those business managers who went through extensive contortions trying to tie the time saved using wireless e-mail applications to specific dollars saved. If users save 11 hours a month processing e-mail, how do you know they will convert x hours of that time into productive work? Sometimes it's enough just to know that people are saving 11 hours.

Determine before you begin the pilot project how much probing and calculating you're going to do to assign dollar values to your ROI, or if your analysis is primarily to put numbers into a business context. Analysis of the latter type might conclude that public works people aren't wasting an hour doing paperwork in the office because of the network, and subsequently they're re-assigned to backlogged projects. No one worries about calculating the specific dollars in productivity savings.

Government department managers who think more like their commercial counterparts may have people and software in place to analyze job performance, productivity, fee-collection cycles, revenue increases and other metrics of successful business operations. If yours doesn't, see if you can borrow these resources from other stakeholders. Before the project begins, try to ensure all stakeholders use the same or similar measurements of broadband's potential and actual impact, time and money saved, contractor agreements impacted and so on that are attributable to the technology. It gives a better picture of the network's overall ROI when everyone's comparing apples to apples.

The Unplanned Benefits May Be the Greater ROI

While job security is definitely enhanced if you deliver on the expected benefits, career advancement certainly gets a boost if you set your analytical sites on uncovering benefits others didn't foresee. To do this, collect a lot of feedback from end users and subscribers in the network's early days of operation, and take a hard look at the data that is coming into the various stakeholder organizations as a result of the network if they're willing to share.

One of the big values broadband applications offer is the potential to change how organizations operate. When you can, anticipate what these changes may be and factor them into the ROI analysis. It's not until people actually use the technology in their jobs can they fully understand its potential. The project team can refine their ROI projections if stakeholders aggressively probe to discover what users are doing that they weren't able to do before deployment.

With social workers carrying laptops to help them process clients' paperwork for city services while at clients' homes, can they also tie into nonprofit agencies' databases to help clients resolve issues with these agencies during the same visit? Can park workers' devices that connect to resources to help them direct tourists to popular destinations also feed summaries of these queries to the chamber of commerce so local retailers can improve their marketing?

Knowledge gathered in real time and properly applied is key to increased constituent satisfaction and more efficient operations. This interlinking of stakeholders knowledge through broadband applications opens the doors to new benefits for stakeholders and their respective constituents. The greater the unexpected ROI from these endeavors, the better your leverage is for getting funding for new applications and infrastructure enhancements.

The future factors into ROI

If your IT staff builds a network architecture that facilitates technology integration including new technologies arriving on the scene, then you have a potential stepping off point for numerous applications to add onto your initial deployment. Where this translates into financial benefits is through time and money savings or new revenue.

Once the network's initial broadband applications deliver benefits that many constituents buy into, you don't have to spend a lot of time selling management and end users on the next applications. People will be coming to you with ideas. From a development standpoint, IT will have an easier time building follow-on applications because a lot of the heavy lifting is done on the initial program. Backend server enhancements, security procedures and hardware and software evaluations, are some of the tasks that should require only rudimentary resource commitments for future projects.

To get a feel for the extent to which you can plan "down the road" ROI potential, use those feedback-gathering interviews with end users to also talk about future applications. Of course, don't overdo the crystal ball gazing with outlandish pie-in-the-sky numbers. Focus projections on applications that can be developed or expanded upon within the next year or two, while giving secondary considerations to applications and technologies that might be three-to-five-years out. As you complete the shorter-term projects, refine your plans as well as estimates on the longer-term applications.

Conduct one or two brainstorming sessions with senior level officials and stakeholders to ponder possible next ventures. This level of buy-in for future plans is helpful if the ROI numbers for the initial implementation are good, but not outstanding. People who can see the big picture view tend to be forgiving if the short term isn't as great as everyone hoped, as long as these visionaries believe the project still has plenty of upside potential.

To Sum It Up

When all is said and done, your ability to measure the return on your investment for broadband infrastructure and applications depends on two things: how clear you are about where you're going, and how well you keep track of results as you get there. The process of doing both of these can be simple or exceedingly complex. There is no universal right or wrong way, though if your community has a good track record implementing technology applications in time and within budget, it's probably good advice to keep those practices in place for broadband.

Be sure to get all of your officials and department managers, stakeholders, constituent groups and even the media on the same page when it comes to your ROI objectives and how these will be quantified after the technology is in place. Maintain a certain amount of flexibility in the ROI analysis process. Use your pilot projects to test and fine-tune ROI assumptions.

Probably the hardest part of any technology deployment comes if someone has to say, "You know, try as hard as we might, we can't get there from here." There are times when the ROI everyone expected or wanted can't be attained with the products, vendors, approach or some other factors currently in place. The politics alone could make this kind of a pronouncement unpalatable. Hopefully someone can make the hard decisions to bring things in line, or throw in the towel if need be. Or you need to work hard to lower people's expectations as you adjust the ROI objectives.

The second hardest thing, at least when deploying broadband for the public good is a primary objective, is quantifying the value of "warm and fuzzy." As Scott Campbell, a Library Director who spearheaded Portsmouth, NH's muni wireless effort, says, "ROI is a tricky thing to measure with a goodwill effort like this. Overall, I see the ROI as a rising-tide-lifts-all-ships type thing. I'm promoting the city of Portsmouth as a viable and vibrant location for forward-minded folks and technology-oriented businesses, and that's good for the entire city."

The important thing here, as with everything else discussed in this book, is that your make decisions which are best for your particular city or county. When you can, rely on other communities and their experiences as guideposts. But ultimately, do what works best for your area.